Contents

Sing Frae the Hert

THE LITERARY CRITICISM
OF
ALEXANDER SCOTT

Selected from the pages of the *Scots Independent*

Introduced and edited by

Neil R MacCallum

SCOTTISH NATIONAL PRESS

published 1996
Scottish Cultural Press
Unit 14, Leith Walk Business Centre, 130 Leith Walk, Edinburgh EH6 5DT
Tel: 0131 555 5950 • Fax: 0131 555 5018

British Library Cataloguing in Publication Data
A catalogue record for this book is available from the British Library

ISBN: 1 898218 70 6

820
M009698

Printed and bound by
Cromwell Press, Melksham, Wiltshire

INTRODUCTION

Alexander Scott was among the most popular and important Scottish writers of his generation; as a poet, playwright, editor and pioneering university teacher of Scottish literature. When his posthumous *Collected Poems* appeared in 1994 (The Mercat Press, edited by David S Robb), I recalled that JB Caird had considered him 'yin o the three skeeliest Lallans makars sin MacDiarmid' and that his fellow poet and playwright Donald Campbell had felt 'there was no anither makar o Alex's generation that's his maik in maistery o the makar's craft ... whenever fowk turn tae poetry for emotion and the sheer joy o sang they'll be shair tae find it in the wark o Alex Scott.' I commented that alongside technical dexterity, linguistic richness and sardonic humour, Scott, whilst rooted in his north-east heritage, 'was able to see it as a building block which would reach out to the wider Scottish and European traditions. He was a writer fully attuned to the challenges and realities of his age.'[1]

It was particularly pleasing for me to receive, shortly thereafter, a thoughtful letter from Scott's widow Cath, recollecting that one of the last judgements Alex had passed on his own poetry firmly 'placed it in the European tradition. You as far as I can tell are the first to acknowledge this point. Throughout our long life together I watched him hone the gift he was given as if it were a precious stone.'[2]

These same qualities were brought to bear on another, sometimes overlooked facet of Scott's considerable output, that of quality literary journalism. Between 13 January 1968 and 28 February 1970, Alex Scott contributed a lively causerie entitled 'Around the Arts', to the then weekly *Scots Independent*. The series had been commissioned by Michael Grieve during his stint as the paper's editor. In all, Scott penned one hundred and eleven pieces, allowing his critical intelligence to take in the whole compass of Scottish cultural endeavour of the period.

JK Annand, harking back to the mid-1920s, was to reminisce about the considerable number of people from a variety of social and occupational backgrounds who had, in increasing numbers, started to buy the *Scottish Educational Journal*.

The explanation for this sudden unexpected popularity of the *Journal* 'among laymen was a series of articles with the general title "Contemporary Scottish Studies", written by one who signed himself as CM Grieve.'[3]

Just over forty years later Annand was to detect a similar phenomenon surrounding the *Scots Independent* wherein Scott 'could be quite devastating in his comments on pretentious writers, but on the other hand, his critical yet kindly appraisals must have given encouragement to numerous up-and-coming authors. The series must have helped to increase the circulation of the paper. I know several people who bought it solely for Scott feature.'[4]

As with the Grieve/MacDiarmid articles, discussion of Scottish literature and language was stimulated and that in itself helped to bring an awareness of quality Scottish writing to a wider constituency than may otherwise have been the case. A fair amount of lively correspondence was generated in the letters page of the paper although coverage of this is unfortunately outwith the scope of the present volume. A full set of all columns, together with this associated correspondence has, however, been lodged with the Scottish Poetry Library in Edinburgh.

It was no easy task to select just thirty of the most representative articles, as all of the contributions seem to have stood the test of time. In making the selection I have attempted to show the breadth of interests covered. Poetry does predominate but that is hardly surprising given Scott's status as a leading poet himself. Sympathy, sincerity and courage tend to be recurring characteristics, for Scott was possessed of an informed approach. A couple of significant examples resulting from this style stand out.

Alan Jackson and Tom Buchan were very much part of an alternative style of Scottish culture in the late 1960s that sometimes sought to reject or debunk the MacDiarmidian literary legacy. Despite being part of the tradition they were often attacking, Scott was able to distance himself from the field of battle to recognise and encourage different sorts of talent when he saw them. Their work is dealt with in the contributions for 28 September 1968 and 31 May 1969. We can also see him picking out, at an early date, emerging writers for whom he accurately predicted fruitful further development. Alastair Mackie on 3 May 1969, John Purser on 10 May 1969, and Donald Campbell on 27 December 1969, were little more than unknown names when some of their early work was picked up by Scott. They all became established personalities in the country's artistic life, although the poet Mackie sadly died last summer following a long illness.

I have felt obliged to exclude from my selection any assessments of various television series as none of the programmes covered is likely to be available to us again. For similar reasons the absence of anything on the visual arts, or the limited space devoted to the theatre (except where general issues were raised), does not mean that these more immediate art forms were neglected by Scott on a week to week basis. I have provided brief biographical notes at the end of each article, along with a list of any books reviewed, and further selective bibliographical details where this would be helpful. I feel confident that the material presented here provides a perceptive snapshot of Scotland's cultural landscape at a defining period in the nation's recent political history. Bernard Tavernier, the French film director, has come out 'against phoney internationalism in films: one should stick to one's cultural roots.'[5] That was a lesson Alex Scott must have learnt long ago.

This selection is being published in November 1996 to mark the seventieth anniversary of the *Scots Independent*'s foundation. The paper first appeared in November 1926 under the auspices of the Scots National League, one of the principal movers behind the National Party of Scotland in 1928, which developed into the modern Scottish National Party in 1934. In his opening editorial William Gillies wrote that, 'It is fitting that, in this our first issue, there should be a brief exposition of the aim and standpoint of the Scots National League. In one sentence – the League's object is the restoration of Scotland to her former position of political independence.'[6]

On the occasion of the paper's fiftieth anniversary in 1976, the then President of the SNP, Dr Robert McIntyre, emphasised that 'the philosophy coming through the pages of these early papers is the same as the philosophy all through the history of the paper ... the main theme is the positive aspiration of people fighting politically for freedom to run their own affairs. Intelligence, sense and human decency come through along with a refusal to be sidetracked and fragmented by ideological claptrap.'

Former SNP chairman, Arthur Donaldson, who wrote for some of these early numbers, recalled that 'it gave valuable publicity to the Scottish Literary Renaissance, then little more than a squalling infant.'[7]

The *SI*, as it became affectionately known, soon made an impact on the Scottish political scene, forcing the ILP-supporting *Forward* to sit up and take notice, and as a result a campaign was launched to defend the record of Scottish Labour MPs.

During most of its early years the paper was the official journal of the NPS, subsequently the SNP, although for a spell it was controlled by the veteran nationalist Roland E Muirhead through his Scottish Secretariat. Since 1955 the *SI* has been established as a separate limited company, associated with and fully supportive of the SNP, but run on behalf of its shareholders by an independent Board of Directors. Kenneth Fee, who has edited the paper since 1985 believes that 'although changes of emphasis are necessary to sustain the paper's continuing relevance in a fluid political climate, our core values and characteristics are still attuned to the cultural strengths identified by our founders.'

When Hugo Claus, one of Belgium's leading twentieth century writers, artists and intellectuals , made the following observations he could actually have been talking about the wider role the *SI* has always strived to achieve in Scottish life and letters: 'The particular precedes the universal and if you want to be particular you are also political because there is nothing that is not political; no-one can say he's outside politics.'[8]

An obligation towards, and an active interest in, promoting Scotland's cultural well-being is immediately apparent to anyone consulting the paper's archives. This is hardly surprising as it emerged from the intellectual climate of the twentieth century Scottish Literary Renaissance spearheaded by Hugh

MacDiarmid. Many prominent writers graced the pages of the *SI* in its early years and throughout the 1930s, with MacDiarmid himself, the poet William Soutar and the novelist Neil Gunn often featuring. Those younger writers, like the poet and polymath Douglas Young, the lyric genius Sydney Goodsir Smith and one Alex Scott, generally described as second wave Renaissance makars start appearing during the war years. One of their number, R Crombie Saunders, went on to edit the paper in the first few years of the 1950s. Goodsir Smith was to edit an attractive *SI* booklet, commemorating the 650th anniversary of the Battle of Bannockburn. AD Mackie, poet, playwright and journalist, who had been a respected figure in Scottish cultural circles since publication of his first book in 1928, held the editorial reins between 1972 and 1974. Donald Campbell took up the mantle of Alex Scott when he penned a regular arts column for the by then revamped and monthly *Scots Independent* from 1974 to 1977. Since taking on the task of arts editor myself at the start of 1991, I have been conscious of joining the company of such distinguished predecessors and hope that their legacy has been well served. Scotland faces exciting times when she should have the opportunity to assert her ancient rights in a new millennium and the *Scots Independent* will be sure to play a part in that historic process.

My thanks are extended to a number of institutions and individuals for their assistance in production of this volume. The Directors of *Scots Independent* (Newspapers) Ltd., were keen supporters of the project from the outset and Peter D Wright, from their number, has been of particular assistance. The staff at both the National Library of Scotland and the Scottish Poetry Library were most helpful. Acknowledgement is made to The Mercat Press, publishers of Alex Scott's *Collected Poems* from which 'Recipe: To Mak a Ballant' is reproduced. Duncan Glen, who was actively involved as a poet and editor during the period dealt with by Scott, read the manuscript and made some useful observations thereon. Jennie Renton, editor of *Scottish Book Collector*, arranged the production of the manuscript with customary efficiency.

It has been a pleasure to work with Jill Dick and Carol Rodger of Scottish Cultural Press who clearly recognised the significance of this selection to Scotland's modern literary history.

Finally, and most importantly I am indebted to Alex's widow, Cath, for her enthusiastic encouragement and valued friendship.

Neil R MacCallum
August 1996

Notes

1. 'On My Word – Around the Arts in Scotland'. Neil R MacCallum, *Scots Independent,* December 1994
2. Letter from Mrs Catherine J Scott of 5 March 1995
3. Review of *Contemporary Scottish Studies* by Hugh MacDiarmid (*Scottish Educational Journal* 1976), JK Annand *Akros* Vol. 11, No. 32, December 1976
4. 'Alexander Scott: An Introduction' – JK Annand, *Akros* Vol. 6, No. 16, April 1971
5. Bernard Tavernier quoted in *France Today.* John Ardagh (Secker & Warburg 1987)
6. 'Scotland a Nation: A Free Land and a Free Folk' *Scots Independent.* No. 1 November 1926
7. *Scots Independent,* fiftieth anniversary issue November 1976
8. Quoted in the Introduction to *Selected Poems 1953–1973,* Hugo Claus, edited by Theo Hermans (Acquila 1986)

RECIPE: TO MAK A BALLANT

To mak a ballant:
tak onie image sclents frae the dark o your mind,
sieve it through twal years' skill
i the fewest words can haud it
(meantime steeran in your hert's bluid),
spice wi wit, saut wi passion,
bile i the hettest fire your love can kindle,
and serve at the scaud in your strangmaist stanza
(the haill process aa to be dune at aince)

Syne rin like hell afore the result explodes!

CORONACH FOR A MAKAR

It wes wi mukkil dule that I read o the daith o yon byornar makar an playwricht – Alexander Scott.

Alang wi makars sic as the umquhile an sairlie missed Sydney Goodsir Smith an Robert Garioch, Alexander Scott mair nor pleyed his pairt in gien a heize in verse ti the guid Scots tongue i the saicont wave o the Scottish Literary Revival. It wes fell fittin that in 1985 he follaed i the fit-steps o Hugh MacDiarmid an Robert McLellan as Honorary Preses o the Scots Language Societie. Throu his daily darg at Glesca Universitie, an his wark for organisations sic as the Association for Scottish Literary Studies, the Saltire Societie an the Scots Language Societie, he did mair nor maist, for ti forder the staunin o Scottish Literature an the Mither Tongue.

Aiblins he wull be best myndit as a makar, bit juist as important wes his darg as Editor o the *Saltire Review* i the fifties; his monie anthologies o Scottish verse, includin a revised edition o *Voices of Our Kind* in 1987; an his wark anent the byous Perth makar William Soutar – a biography *Still Life*, an the editin o Soutar's byornar *Diaries of a Dying Man*. Throu the acktivities o the Association for Scottish Literary Studies, whilk he served as Secretar an syne Preses, he made siccar that monie negleckit Scottish literary classics hae bin reprentit an gien thair richtfu place i our nation's lyf.

Born in Aiberdeen in 1920, Alexander Scott wes commissioned i the Gordon Highlanders durin the Hitler Weir. He wes woundit at Normandy an awardit the Military Cross. He peyed braw tribute ti his deid comrades in 'Coronach – for the deid o the 5th/7th Battalion, The Gordon Highlanders' –

> Waement the deid
> I never did,
> Owre gled I was ane o the lave
> That somewey baid alive
> To trauchle my thowless hert
> Wi ithers' hurt
>
> But nou that I'm far
> Frae the fechtin's fear,

Nou I hae won awa frae aa thon pain
Back til my beuks and my pen,
They croud aroun me out o the grave
Whaur love and langourie sae lanesome grieve.

Cryan the cauld words:
'We hae dree'd our weirds,
But you that byde ahin,
Ayont our awesome hyne,
You are the flesh we aince had been,
We that are bruckle brokken bane.'

Efter the Weir he raturnt ti Aiberdeen Universitie, afore stertin a
Universitie career at Embro, an syne Glesca Universitie whaur he wes
Heid o the Depairtment o Scottish Literature.

He wes na cringin Scot. He ettled, lyk Hugh MacDiarmid, ti sen the
Suddron 'reid roses, back ayont the Border' for

We hae a rose o our ain:
Unhapped frae the dark til the sheen o the sun,
Bonnie she'll blaw her lane.

He wes teuch and straucht ti the pynt, granite-lyk, bit he cuid aye
finn a place for a bittie uimour. Aulder readers wull mynd that frae the
brae ouklie airts skreed he countributit ti the SI during late 1960s.

Maist o his poetrie wes skrcivit i Scots, an nane better nor the television poem til the Granite City – 'Heart of Stone' – published in *Cantrips*
in 1968.

A teuch toun, whaur even the strand maks sillar,
A rouch Riveera gley at the granite sea,
Wi a fun-fair squatteran roun the Muckle Dipper,
A sprauchle o stalls for sweeties and ice-a-da-cream
To fleech til the tongues o bairns o a fause simmer
And cant o the sun til bonnie bare-buff quines
On a bourached beach whaur crouds find crouseness in crouds,
Cantie to keek at the quines –

He claucht weill the virr an birr o his native leid, an whitna Scot
cuidna bit finn thaimsels at hame wi a swatch or twa frae his uimourous
keeks at the foibles o our fella Scots i the series o satyrical epigrams
Scotched.

Scotch Equality
Kaa the feet frae
Thon big bastard.

Scotch Optimism
Through a gless,
Darkly.

Scotch Pessimism
Nae
Gless.

Scotch Education
I tellt ye
I tellt ye.

Makars sic as Alexander Scott hae addit ti the walth an varietie o Scottish lyf an culture, for athout the wark o our makars, airtists, an playwrichts, the hale qualitie o lyf in Scotland wad be mukkil the puirer. The airts bring ure an bonnieness ti lyf, an Alexander Scott for monie a yeir ettelt athwarts that end.

Weill is he wordie o his place in Scottish literature – his wark assurit o a place i our kintra's abydin heritage. Scotland, on the fowreteint o September, lost a leal son, the Scottish cause a bonnie fechter an a guid fier. Lyk William Dunbar i the saxteint centurie we can aw lament for a Scottish makar – Alexander Scott (1920–1989).

(Peter D Wright, *Scots Independent* November 1989)

13 January 1968

Iain Cuthbertson, the new director of the Perth Theatre, wrote recently about 'Scotland's most popular dramatic tradition – front-cloth comedy.' He was referring to pantomime.

That was in November, at the beginning of Perth's excitingly experimental all-Scottish season. Now the festive season is upon us. But where are the Scottish pantomimes?

Perth, following the tradition established by the Glasgow Citizens' Theatre with *The Tintock Cup*, are presenting a version of *Cinderella* created by the company specifically for Scottish audiences. In this they seem to be unique among the repertory theatres supported by grants from the Scottish Arts Council.

Instead of 'Scotland's most popular dramatic tradition,' Glasgow Citizens' Christmas show is a revival of that corny old English farce, *Rookery Nook*. In Edinburgh, the Lyceum has *Toad of Toad Hall* and the Traverse *Waiting for Godot*.

All good clean fun, of course. And all already successful in foreign parts. But this is the time of the year when even the Scots have been prepared to go to the theatre *en masse* and enjoy comic representations – or misrepresentations – of themselves. Why are they no longer given the chance?

It may well be that the producers and actors at the Citizens', the Lyceum and the Traverse are constitutionally incapable of presenting Scottish material, most – if not all – of them being resident aliens. Should that be so, then most – if not all – of them have resided here too long.

This is not to suggest that the Scottish Arts Council should support only those rep theatres which present Scottish plays and Scottish plays alone. But serious consideration should be given to the withdrawal of Scottish subsidies from companies so dominated by Sassenachs that Scottish dialogue is beyond their tongues and Scottish themes beneath their interest.

It wasn't so long ago that the only literary magazine in Scotland was *Lines*, the poetry review, and even this staggered out so infrequently, once a year at most, that it could give only a belated impression of the continuing development of Scottish verse.

Happily those days are now over. *Lines,* with a Scottish Arts Council grant, is able to appear twice a twelvemonth and *Akros*, which Duncan Glen has been publishing three times a year since 1965, has also received a grant from the same source which has enabled it to double its size.

In the latest *Akros*, which appeared in December, all the poems are in Scots, and in his editorial Duncan Glen seems to be throwing down a challenge to the editors of *Scottish Poetry* – the annual anthology published by Edinburgh University Press – and the editor of *Lines*. He suggests that these have no real interest in encouraging younger poets writing in Scots, although they 'have been able to appear non-cliqueish by printing Scots work by established writers.'

What are the facts behind this charge? In *Scottish Poetry 2* (1967), there are five poems – 15 pages – in Scots as against eighty-five poems – 100 pages – in English; and three of the five Scots poets are 'established writers' (in the sense of appearing in most anthologies).

In *Lines 25* there are four poems – seven pages – in Scots as against eighteen poems – eighteen pages – in English, and all the Scots poets are 'established writers.' In *Akros 6*, on the other hand, there are twenty-two poems in Scots, and only two of the contributors are 'established writers' in the sense given above.

Does Duncan Glen's charge stand proven, then? Yes and no.

Some of the poems in *Akros* by Scots writers who are not yet 'established' are as good as any of those in *Scottish Poetry* and *Lines* by established makars. Others, however, are worse. Some are much worse – even much, much worse. Yet the question arises – are these Scots beginners at all inferior to some of the English apprentices who have featured in *Scottish Poetry* and *Lines*? As a poet who has appeared in anthologies in both languages, I am compelled to say that they aren't.

What emerges from this controversy is that the younger, non-established poets writing in Scots lack confidence in the editorial board of *Scottish Poetry*, since it does not contain a poet whose reputation rests on his work in Scots.

Iain Cuthbertson (1930–). Actor; director, Perth Theatre 1967–1968. General Manager and Director of Productions Citizens' Theatre Glasgow 1962–1965.

Lines Review, founded 1952, published by M Macdonald (Edinburgh, later Loanhead, various editors)

Akros, 1965–1983, editor Duncan Glen, published by Akros Publications, (Glasgow, later Preston and then Nottingham).

Scottish Poetry. Annual volume 1966–1976. (Nos. 1–6, editors George Bruce, Maurice Lindsay, Edwin Morgan (Edinburgh University Press).

No. 7, editors Maurice Lindsay, Alexander Scott, Roderick Watson (University of Glasgow Press).

Nos. 8-9, editors Maurice Lindsay, Alexander Scott, Roderick Watson (Carcanet).

27 January 1968

At long, long last, after years and years of total silence, one of the established Scottish publishing houses has got round to putting out a collection of verse by one of the established Scottish poets.

This kind of earth-shaking event hasn't happened here for nine songless years. Not since 1959. Then the publishers were Oliver and Boyd – at that time still independent, and still Scottish.

The poet was Sydney Goodsir Smith, who writes in Scots. The book was *Figs and Thistles*, a highly individual collection.

Now the publishers are the Edinburgh University Press, one of the few houses in this country still independent.

The poet is Edwin Morgan, who writes in English. The book is *The Second Life*, a highly individual collection.

Morgan, on the strength of his best work, may well come to be regarded as the finest poet ever to emerge from Glasgow and to make that smoky cityscape the main theme of some of his most powerful verse.

The cry of human agony that is 'Glasgow Green' pierces through the provincial scene to achieve universality. Scarcely less intense in the passion of its pity is 'King Billy' on the burial of a Glasgow gangleader. But such is Morgan's versatility that he can write equally successful comic poems too. 'The Starlings in George Square' is hilariously funny in its description of the effect those shrill wings make on the 'Lord Provost in her marble hacienda' and on lesser mortals compelled to go about their business while the birds are doing theirs.

In his best love poems, again, Morgan is tender and yet never trite. 'One Cigarette', with its vivid first line, 'No smoke without you, my fire', has that moving simplicity which only high talent can achieve.

Morgan is also a poet of fantastic imagination, who delights in the exploration of outer space – and inner space – as expressed in science-fiction. Some of his poems on such themes are 'way out' in every sense of that phrase. To me they represent a significant extension of poetry's imaginative range.

About other 'way out' aspects of *The Second Life* there may be less appreciation. It all depends on whether one can accept so-called 'concrete' work as poetry. I can't.

Some of Morgan's successful poems – and some of his failures too – originally appeared in the annual anthology *Scottish Poetry* which he edits for Edinburgh University Press with George Bruce and Maurice Lindsay. This editorial trio have shown admirable range of taste in the two collections hitherto published. They have avoided clique controversies, and instead have sought out the best in every school of Scottish verse.

Morgan is also a member of the editorial board of the new cultural quarterly, *Scottish International*, which is due to appear for the first time on 26 January. Here too, a considerable variety of contributors has been assembled.

Since *Scottish International* and *Scottish Poetry* are subsidised by the Scottish Arts Council, they should become permanent features of what passes for our cultural life. Every writer in Scotland is bound to wish them well. Yet it's impossible to feel entirely happy about the presence of the same man on the editorial boards of both publications. This means that the writer whose work is rejected by one of these periodicals cannot feel free to offer it to the other. Such restraint upon artistic liberty is deplorable. It ought to be removed immediately.

Also published this month with a Scottish Arts Council subsidy is the latest number of *Lines Review*, edited by young Edinburgh poet Robin Fulton and including verse in English, Scots and Gaelic.

In addition to fine poems by Goodsir Smith, Robert Garioch, DM Black, Edwin Morgan and Tom Scott, this issue has some promising apprentice work in verse.

In prose, there is a controversial article by Douglas Young on Hugh MacDiarmid's even more controversial *Collected Poems* and the reviews range from discrimination by Norman MacCaig to denunciation by Alan Bold. In future, *Lines* is to appear three times a year instead of just twice yearly as at present. The other Scottish poetry magazine *Akros*, edited by the critic Duncan Glen, is published quarterly.

Did someone say 'There are more magazines than makars?' The makars will reply, 'The more the merrier.'

Edwin Morgan (1920–). Poet, critic and translator. Emeritus Professor of English, University of Glasgow.
The Second Life: Selected Poems (Edinburgh University Press 1968)
Collected Poems (Carcanet 1990; revised edition 1995).

10 February 1968

London has won another victory. But this time, for once, London has won for Scotland.

In the same month that has seen the publication, in Edinburgh, of a new cultural quarterly with the question-begging title *Scottish International,* London has launched the biggest and brightest Scottish magazine to appear since the war.

The current number of *Agenda,* edited in London by William Cookson with a grant from the Arts Council of Great Britain, is a double issue, entirely concerned with the twin topics of 'Hugh MacDiarmid and Scottish Poetry'.

A magazine which starts with MacDiarmid's moving poem, 'Bracken Hills in Autumn', and continues with another 12 pages of the Michty Makar's vehemently characteristic verse takes a risk of beginning with a bang but ending with a whimper.

Agenda meets the challenge and surmounts it in fine style. The eight articles on the inexhaustible variety of MacDiarmid's work are written with verve and enthusiasm, even when the critics find themselves doubting the success of one or other aspect of the great man's work. The contributors themselves are as various as their views. They include poets, scholars and professional critics. Some are Scots, some Irish, some English.

Tell of it not in Gath, publish it not in the streets of Askelon – but in its 60 pages of prose, *Agenda* shows itself more worthy of the name *Scottish International* than the magazine which flaunts that title before our 'narrowly nationalistic' eyes.

The 30-page selection of contemporary Scottish verse which concludes the issue has been made by Tom Scott, and the standard is so consistently high that it's almost invidious to choose for special mention the poems by Norman MacCaig, Robin Fulton and Iain Crichton Smith, writing in English, and those of Robert Garioch, AD Mackie and Tom Scott himself, writing in Scots.

Scott's savagely satirical attack on the City Fathers of Edinburgh, whom he sees as wicked stepfathers rather than as true parents, shows that the old flyting tradition can rise far above the medieval level of personal abuse without losing anything of the fine cutting edge of its scorn.

The poem faces, on the opposite page, Robin Fulton's 'A Calvinist in Spite of Himself'. A Scottish Everyman? Fulton skates across the thin ice of his subject with dazzling dexterity.

Although the matter of Gaelic poetry is touched on in an article on MacDiarmid's 'Lament for the Great Music,' there are no Gaelic poems in *Agenda.* This is unfortunate, since MacDiarmid has had his influence upon modern Gaelic poets as well as on those of us who write in English or Scots. The omission is all the more regrettable when Derick Thomson, writing in Gaelic, has emerged in his most recent work as one of our finest poets, superb alike in satire and in sorrow.

His latest collection, published last year, is *Eadar Samhradh is Foghar,* a title which is a poem in itself: 'Between Summer and Autumn'. Along with 50 poems in Gaelic, Thomson also publishes 26 of them in English versions. Even in translation these read brilliantly. In the original they must be magnificent.

Yet two out of the three literary periodicals edited by Lowland Scots and concerned with the art of poetry have so far passed by Thomson's book in silence.

The honourable exception is *Akros,* edited by Duncan Glen. The current issue contains a sensitive appreciation of modern Gaelic poetry, including Thomson's latest volume, by Iain Crichton Smith – himself one of the few writers to achieve equal excellence in both Gaelic and English.

In the current issue of *Lines Review,* edited by Robin Fulton, Thomson's Gaelic poem on Lewis is powerfully evocative. The absence of any review of his book is made all the more notable thereby.

The first issue of *Scottish International* finds room for a three-column review of anthologies of the current concrete-mixing craze which most Scottish poets regard with the contempt it deserves.

Other three-column reviews discuss volumes of verse by a brace of beginners, the talented DM Black and the turbulent Alan Bold, both of whom write in English. Mrs Edith Anne Robertson, who writes in Scots, receives one column only for the discussion of her *Collected Ballads and Poems.* Derick Thomson, in Gaelic, receives not even a mention.

For *Scottish International* it's evident that internationalism does NOT begin at home.

Tom Scott (1918–1995). Poet and literary scholar.
The Ship and Ither Poems (Oxford University Press 1963)
Dunbar – a critical exposition of the poems (Oliver and Boyd 1966)
The Collected Shorter Poems of Tom Scott (Agenda/Chapman Publications 1993)

Derick Thomson (*Ruaraidh MacThòmais*) (1921–). Poet. Editor of *Gairm* since 1952. Professor of Celtic, University of Glasgow 1963–1990.
Eadar Samthradh is Foghar (Gairm 1967)
Creachadh na Clàrsaich – Plundering the Harp – Collected Poems 1940–1980 (Macdonald 1982)

Edith Anne Robertson (1889-1975). Poet and translator.
Collected Poems and Ballads in the Scots Tongue with an introduction by Douglas Young (Aberdeen University Press 1969)

Agenda. Literary quarterly founded 1959. Double issue Autumn/Winter 1967/1968 'Hugh MacDiarmid and Scottish poetry' edited by William Cookson, in collaboration with Tom Scott.

Scottish International 1968–1974 (quarterly, monthly from May 1971). Editors: Robert Tait 1968–1973; Tom Buchan 1973–1974; editorial advisers Robert Garioch and Edwin Morgan.

Through the hurricanes of laughter at the gala performance of the Glasgow Citizens' production of *The Anatomist*, performed to raise funds for the Duncan Macrae memorial theatre, there sounded in my ear a sardonic chuckle. The voice seemed to have the authentic tone of dear dead Duncan.

The Anatomist was described by its author, James Bridie, as 'a lamentable comedy.' That phrase is no less applicable to the post-mortem movement to honour the memory of Macrae.

Duncan Macrae was the greatest Scottish actor of his time. Yet the blaze of his genius was scarcely ever given the opportunity to set the heather on fire. Each time smoke rose above a kindling crackle of flame, it was dashed out by buckets of cold water from the brigade who regarded Scottishness as dangerous incendiarism.

Throughout the quarter-century of his professional career Macrae scintillated from the stages of all our principal theatres. But Scotland failed to provide the theatre where his immense ability in our own indigenous style would have the chance of continuous development and growing influence.

Where he should have been at the centre of a Scottish dramatic movement, Macrae was manoeuvred out to the circumference. The fact that he was a great performer in a uniquely Scottish mode was regarded as a limiting weakness rather than a quickening source of strength.

He emerged as the brightest star of our stage at the Glasgow Citizens' during that theatre's heroic age, its first decade, before the death of its founding father, Bridie. But the magnificent figure's rather less splendid successors were either unwilling or unable develop the dramatic situation which had come into being as the result of Macrae's achievement of stardom.

Instead of becoming the lynch-pin of Citizens' policy, Macrae left the company. But in the Scotland of that period, there was nowhere else he could go but into pantomime. If Sir Laurence Olivier could find no other way of exercising his talent than by giving comic recitations at the Palladium, the waste of superb capabilities would be no greater.

Macrae's tours with his own company during summer seasons provided no substitute for the permanent Scottish theatre he wished to see, the national theatre with a considerable proportion of Scottish plays in its repertoire and a high percentage of Scottish actors among its players.

While Macrae was touring, the Citizens' stood still, trying to find a policy. The liaison which had been established between that theatre and Scottish dramatists was lost and the voice of Scotland was drowned by the London accent.

Occasionally Macrae was invited back to the Citizens' as 'guest star', but he was as likely to be required to appear in some English play giving little or no scope for his native talents as in some indigenous work included in a largely English repertoire as a sop to Scottish feeling.

Conditions in the other reps offered Macrae no greater scope. Dundee and Perth were little more than provincial branches of the London establishment, and in Edinburgh the Gateway, thirled to the kirk, was too cautious to be able to capture the younger generation.

When Macrae was struck down by the first symptoms of a fatal illness, he was rehearsing with the Lyceum Company in Edinburgh. The play was *Treasure Island*, the part Long John Silver. A popular play in the English cloak-and-dagger tradition, a meaty part in the style of English skulduggery – but no more appropriate to Macrae's essentially Scottish genius than Kew Gardens to the thistle.

Now that Macrae is dead, the Citizens' helps to raise funds towards the establishment of the kind of Scottish theatre for which he sought in vain during his lifetime. But in order to present that eminently Scottish play *The Anatomist,* the Citizens' has had to draw upon talents which otherwise find all too few opportunities on its stage today.

The guest producer is that great Ulsterman, Sir Tyrone Guthrie, once of the Scottish National Players. Among the actors who have returned to the Citizens' for this particular production after too many months and years of absence are Edith Macarthur, Jean Taylor-Smith, James Gibson, Roddy MacMillan and John Grieve. The leading role is played by the eminent Edinburgh 'stranger,' Tom Fleming, who gives a brilliant performance.

If the Citizens' were performing its proper function, such actors would be permanent members of the company. But the present régime in that particular theatre is far too intent on appearing 'international' – i.e. English with a few continental trimmings – to provide work for Scottish players.

John Duncan Grahame Macrae (1905–1967). Actor and theatre director. Described by the playwright Donald Campbell as 'the greatest Scottish actor'. Dedicated to the cause of Scottish theatre.

Wise Enough to Play the Fool: *A Biography of Duncan Macrae* Priscilla Barlow (John Donald 1995)

23 March 1968

With the death of Sir Alexander Gray at the ripe old age of 85, Scotland has lost a great scholar and a fine poet.

His poetical achievement was built over some forty years of endeavour, beginning with *Songs and Ballads chiefly from Heine* in 1920 and ending – at least so far as publication was concerned – with *Historical Ballads of Denmark* in 1958.

Between those dates there were four other volumes of translation, a book of *Selected Poems* and two volumes of his original verse in Scots and English.

Through all the vagaries of poetical taste between 1920 and today, Sir Alexander never lost his hold upon the public, and his fellow poets continued to read him with admiration.

Even his earliest work remains as delightfully alive now as when first composed all those decades ago.

> You say you dinna lo'e me Jean?
> That winna gar me dee.
> Just let me see your bonny een,
> And wha sae blithe as me?
> I hear your bonny reid lips say
> You hate me, lass! O fie!
> Just let me kiss them nicht and day –
> And what the deil care I?

In that version of Heine, and in most others, Sir Alexander succeeded in transferring the lyrical impulse from German into Scots with scarcely a grain of loss in impact, emotional truth, and lyrical quality. Although he transformed Heine into a Scot, his art was so skilfully translucent that the personality of the original writer still shone through.

With his very first book, Sir Alexander at once took his place in the great tradition of Scottish translators, the golden chain which has glittered through our literary history from medieval to modern times.

In his later work, Sir Alexander translated from a varied and vigorous range of folksong and balladry in German, Dutch and Danish, and nine times out of ten his versions had such authenticity of feeling and tone that they read like indigenous Scottish songs.

His comic ballad 'The Hey' is from the German yet it has all the gallus humour, the coarse wit of that anonymous Scottish masterpiece, 'Our gudeman cam hame at e'en'.

Again, that tender pathos which shimmers like unshed tears in so many of our love-songs, finds a rare delicacy of expression in 'The Dream', another translation of a German original.

> A' nicht lang I hae dreamit,
> A heavy dream for me.
> There grew within my gairden
> A tree o'rosemary.
> The gairden was a kirkyaird;
> A grave, the bed o' flowers.
> And blumes and leaves throughither
> Fell frae the tree in showers.

In writing original poetry in Scots, Sir Alexander limited himself to 'those things which make up the lives of those who naturally speak in dialect,' and as a result he found that he was 'forced ... to go back to his village ... and project himself into the life which he might have led there.'

But if a sophisticated scholar consciously plays the character part of a rural rhymer there is likely to be some incongruity in the performance.

It is only when Sir Alexander draws upon his experience of contemporary city life, as in 'Babylon in Retrospect', that his original Scots verse moves beyond pastiche into poetry, with its own individual voice.

In English, Sir Alexander is best-known for his patriotic poem, 'Scotland', which opens with a beautifully-spare evocation of his native landscape –

> Here in the uplands
> The soil is ungrateful;
> The fields red with sorrell,
> Are stony and bare.
> A few trees, wind-twisted –
> Or are they but bushes?
> Stand stubbornly guarding
> A home here and there.

Unfortunately, this high level of 'eye-on-the-object' writing is not maintained in the concluding stanzas of this work which has suffered from over-exposure in the anthologies.

My own preference is for 'Age', a poem equally patriotic, but where the patriotism finds an expression which is at once deeper and quieter and all the more moving for the utter absence of any suggestion of striving for effect.

> A barren soil I tilled for bread,
> When Alexander our King was dead,
> And in my flesh I bear concealed
> Bannockburn and Flodden Field.

An accomplished poet is dead. His work lives.

Sir **Alexander Gray** (1882–1968). Poet and translator. Professor of Political Economy, University of Aberdeen, 1921–1934, University of Edinburgh 1934–1956.

Songs and Ballads, Chiefly from Heine (The Richard Press 1920)
Gossip (Porpoise Press 1928)
Selected Poems, edited by Maurice Lindsay (William Maclellan 1948)
Historical Ballads of Denmark (Edinburgh University Press 1958)

6 April 1968

Legend tells us of that ornithological oddity, the ooja-ooja bird, which is reputed to pass its incredible existence in flying round and round in ever-decreasing circles, until it suddenly vanishes inside its own being in a manner at once intimate, miraculous and messy.

Novels written by literary apprentices about literary apprentices writing novels I have hitherto regarded as belonging to the ooja-ooja school of fiction, as self-swallowing monstrosities, to be marvelled at as weird wonders rather than appreciated as natural creations.

Fortunately, there are exceptions to every rule, even the most irregular. Archie Hind's book, *The Dear Green Place*, is highly exceptional.

When he wrote this work, Mr Hind was a literary apprentice – it first appeared in 1966, under the imprint of New Authors Ltd. – and he was concerned with a hero who not only tried (and failed) to write a novel but went on to try (and fail) with another.

Unpromising material, it might appear, for the general reader. But in this case appearances are even more deceptive than usual.

Far from its interest being limited only to those who are themselves of a literary turn of mind, *The Dear Green Place* – which has just been reissued in paperback – makes a wide appeal by the accuracy of its observation of the hero's environment and the sympathy and skill of its characterisation both of the apprentice-novelist himself and of the other folk, family and friends, with whom he is involved.

The nature of the environment is indicated, ironically, by the book's title – for 'the dear green place' is, of course, the translation of the original Gaelic phrase from which derives the place-name of that city which is as often dreary as dear, and more widely grimy than green – Glasgow.

Like Mr Hind himself, his hero Mat Craig might claim the song 'I belong to Glasgow' as his own urban anthem. But Craig – again like the author – is aware that the notorious ditty tells not even a quarter, let alone half of the truth about a town whose complexities and contradictions have been at least as much the despair as the delight of every writer who has attempted to express them.

'A city whose talents were all outward and acquisitive. Its huge mad Victorian megalomaniac art gallery full of acquired art, its literature dumb or in exile, its poetry a dull struggle in obscurity, its night-life non-existent, its theatres unsupported, its Sundays sabbatarian, its secular life moderate and dull on the one hand and sordid, furtive and predatory on the other'.

But if author and hero alike are repelled by many aspects of their birth-place, there are others which fascinate them, and it is out of the tension created by this love-hate relationship that the vibration of the book's appeal arises.

'A dirty filthy city,' Mr Hind calls Glasgow, with the brusque bluntness of the native-born. 'But', he is compelled to add, 'with a kind of ample vitality which has created fame for her slums and her industry and given her moral and spiritual existence a tight ingrown wealth, like a human character, limited, but with a direct brutish strength, almost warm.'

Knowing that 'tight ingrown wealth, like a human character' from the inside, Mr Hind also knows the actual human characters who embody it, the artisans and the labourers among whom he was born and grew up, 'the five-eights,' as the hero's brother calls himself and them. And because he is one of them, he is able to present each as a unity rather than as the just-more than-half-man indicated by the brother's deprecatory self-description.

The hero's failure to write his two novels derives from the deprivations he suffered from being born and brought up in a slum in a city unconcerned with fostering aesthetic sensibility. But although *The Dear Green Place* seems to end in failure, every reader realises that the actual conclusion has been a success.

For this is an autobiographical novel, where the hero resembles the author so closely as to be regarded as his representative. And the author-hero, after his first two failures, went on to try and try again until his trials eventuated in the triumph of *The Dear Green Place* itself.

The undefeatable determination which brought about this victory must have its source in Mr Hind's own character. But if novelists, like poets, are born and not made, they are inevitably conditioned by their place of birth, the traditions they inherit, and the scenes among which they reach maturity.

Glasgow gave Mr Hind its 'ample vitality', the fierce energy of those generations of workers who had to fight to live, and he himself possessed the artist's seeing eye through which he has been able to penetrate the grime of an unlovely environment and attain appreciation of the green oases of love and indomitability.

He has written a book which, like his native city, is both harsh and humorous, both violent and vital. The sensitivity of the writing is his own achievement.

Archie Hind (1928–). Novelist and playwright.
> *The Dear Green Place* (New Authors 1966); paperback edition 1968; (reprinted Polygon 1984)

27 April 1968

The chapter of autobiography by George Bruce which appears in the current issue of *Scottish International* should throw a flood of light on a writer whose work reflects with masterful accuracy the environment in which he grew up and the folk who lived there.

Bruce was born and brought up in and around Fraserburgh, a region which has not yet been swamped by the cosmopolitan pseudo-culture of the world's great cities. In the North-East, the people are still a community rather than a mob of strangers, and the communal consciousness informs much of Bruce's best verse.

Born in 1909, Bruce came of a family which had been settled in Fraserburgh for at least a hundred years, during which time it had been closely identified with the fishing industry which dominates the town's economy and the way of life of its folk.

His great-grandfather founded the firm of A. Bruce & Co., Herring Curers, at the beginning of the nineteenth century, and it remained a family concern until the death of the poet's father in 1941.

As a member of such a family, Bruce early became aware of the community in which he lived, for that community was an extension of the family group, sharing the same interests, their lives centred on the same always-dramatic conflict, man's battle to wrest a living from the dangerous sea.

In his poem, 'Inheritance', Bruce describes the influence of the family tradition upon his work,

> Seamen and craftsmen and curers,
> And behind them
> The protest of hundreds of years,
> The sea obstinate against the land.

This is the 'matter' of Bruce's verse. In his best poetry we seem to hear more than an individual voice, we listen to the voice of a whole community, the folk among whom the poet achieved maturity and with whom he shares a width and depth of experience.

Not that Bruce's work is impersonal in style – on the contrary, his style is one of the most individual to be found among contemporary Scottish poets. But it is different from other contemporary styles as his subject-matter is different, since it is a style peculiarly fitted to his themes.

'His poetry', as one perceptive critic commented, 'by avoiding inessentials which would blur the precise outline seeks to epitomise something of the physical nature of the East Coast of Scotland and something of the spirit of the people who live and work there.'

Whatever else may be said about the North-East coast, it can scarcely be described as conventionally pretty. Bare strength, resistance, endurance – those are the qualities of the coast-line which impress themselves upon the observer – and they are, essentially, the qualities of Bruce's verse.

> This is the outermost edge of Buchan.
> Inland the sea birds range,
> The tree's leaf has salt upon it,
> The tree turns to the low stone wall …
> The water plugs in the cliff sides,
> The gull cries from the clouds

That passage is as stark, and as impressive, as the scene it describes, the directness of the style reflecting the nakedness of stone and sky, the slow, abrupt rhythms echoing the assault of the sea against the cliff and the steady endurance of the rock which goes on forever 'rejecting the violence of water.'

Bruce's approach to poetry-making is revealed in one of his poems on another art, 'The Sculptor', where he writes –

> The sculptor, revealing by his skill
> Shape and line and plane, ignoring beauty, makes it.

Since Bruce deals with a landscape impressed upon his imagination in childhood, and with people whom he regards as belonging to a larger family of which his own forms part, his emotions are directly involved in his writing, and it is this emotional force which 'makes beauty' out of his concern with 'shape and line and plane,' welding the particular observations into unity.

His latest collection, *Landscapes and Figures*, was published six months ago by Akros Publications. The title exactly indicates the nature of the contents.

Bruce has provided 'a local habitation and a name' for universal qualities, and created a landscape and a people embodying the eternal virtues of courage and endurance.

George Bruce (1909–). Poet, critic and lecturer. BBC Radio Producer
  1946–1970.
  Sea Talk (Maclellan 1944)
  Landscapes and Figures (Akros Publications 1967)
  Collected Poems (Edinburgh University Press 1971)
  Perspectives: Poems 1970–1986 (Aberdeen University Press 1987)

25 May 1968

Driving along a twistily-twining country road through the green depths of rural Angus the other weekend, we passed a sign that said 'Noranside', and my wife and I exchanged glances and made a simultaneous exclamation, 'Helen Cruickshank country!'

What we had in mind, of course, was the title of Miss Cruickshank's first collection of verse, *Up the Noran Water*, published in 1934, and the poem from which that title derives, 'Shy Geordie', the lovely and lively lyric which tellingly expresses the idiosyncratic amalgam of coorseness and tenderness in the Scottish character.

> Up the Noran Water,
> In by Inglismaddy,
> Annie's got a bairnie
> That hasna got a daddy …
> But oh! the bairn at Annie's breist,
> The love in Annie's ee!
> They mak me wish wi' a' my micht
> The lucky lad was me!

When we got home from our weekend, the post brought us Helen Cruickshank's latest book of poems, *The Ponnage Pool*, published by M Macdonald of Edinburgh, to coincide with the celebrations of the author's 82nd birthday on May 15.

Here is a selection of the best work Miss Cruickshank has produced during a poetical career which has already spanned half a century and which shows no sign of slackening yet – the most recent poem in the book, 'Elegy for Susie', a moving lament for the death of a young girl ('Fingers too frail to grasp life's nettle whole'), is dated 18 January 1968.

Together with 36 poems from Miss Cruickshank's two earlier books – the latter of which, *Sea Buckthorn*, appeared in 1954 – the new volume contains 17 previously unpublished poems, most of them written since her 70th birthday.

The intellectual energy and the passionate potency in these poems would be remarkable in a writer of any age. From a poet who has long since marched past the Biblical milestone of three-score years and ten, they are beyond praise.

Miss Cruickshank's width of range is as notable in style as in subject matter moving from the 'concrete' manner in 'Peradventure', where the shape of the poem on the page is essential to its total effect, to an adaptation of Alexander Mongomerie's sixteenth-century Scots in 'A Lang Guidnicht', a moving meditation on the plight of Scotland which is at the same time a call to action.

Other political poems, in both Scots and English, bear witness to the octogenarian poet's continuing concern with the issue of death or resurrection for this country – a concern which makes her contemporary, for all her years, with the youngest of Scotland's new generation of activists.

But her finest poems transcend politics and concentrate the essence of themes of universal relevance, youth and age, the challenge which death presents to the individual spirit and the undying endeavour of art.

That Miss Cruickshank's best work is destined to live as long as the Scottish tradition in literature I haven't the slightest doubt for she has written some of the loveliest lyrical poetry, tempering the masculine strength of craftsmanship with the feminine delicacy of insight, which it has ever been my privilege and pleasure to read.

Her masterpiece, in my opinion, is the title poem of the present volume, 'The Ponnage Pool', where the mysterious intermingledom of life and death is poignantly expressed through the images of salmon-fishing in her native river, the Esk – a work which is at once local and universal, rooted in everyday reality and yet shining with the unearthly radiance of more-than-mortal vision.

> I am the deep o' the pule,
> The fish, the fisher.
> The river in spate,
> The broon o' the far peat-moss
> The shingle bricht wi' the flooer
> O' the yellow mim'lus,
> The martin fleein' across.

More than a quarter of a century has passed since I first read this superb evocation of the miraculous inter-relationship of the ephemeral and the eternal, and I believe that the poem will prove to be as immortal as the experience it expresses.

But Miss Cruickshank's insight has not dimmed with age. One of the most recent poems in the new collection is 'Epistle for Christopher Murray Grieve on his 75th Birthday', written only a year ago, and what she says here about Hugh MacDiarmid might be applied with equal justice to herself

> Yer poems spring as fresh as till ye strive
> Tae kep their glisk thro drumlie darkness brakin

Again, in 'Primroses for a Birthday', written in 1966, Miss Cruickshank pays graceful tribute to her predecessors in the long honour-roll of Scottish poets. Those of us who are young enough to be able to hold Helen Cruickshank among our own predecessors are fortunate in the inspiration of her work and her example.

Helen B Cruickshank (1886–1975). Poet, longstanding friend of Hugh MacDiarmid – Dr CM Grieve – whom she succeeded as Secretary of Scottish PEN in 1927 serving until 1934.
Up the Noran Water (Methuen 1934)
Sea Buckthorn (HT Macpherson 1954)
The Ponnage Pool (Macdonald 1968)
Collected Poems (Reprographia 1971)

1 June 1968

Since his emergence in the mid-twenties as modern Scotland's greatest writer, Hugh MacDiarmid has been regarded as a father-figure by a whole generation of younger poets, to whom his example has been a constant source of encouragement even in the most discouraging circumstances.

MacDiarmid's own father-figure, however, was not a poet but a schoolmaster – George Ogilvie who was principal teacher of English in the Pupil Teacher Centre at Broughton in Edinburgh when 16-year-old Christopher Murray Grieve arrived there from his native Langholm with 'a Border accent you could have cut with a knife.'

It was to Ogilvie that Grieve-MacDiarmid dedicated 'A Moment in Eternity', the earliest of his verses to be included in his *Collected Poems*, and throughout his career he has frequently acknowledged the stimulating effect which the width and depth of Ogilvie's intellectual and literary interests had upon him during his student days.

But that stimulus endured for many years after Grieve had ceased to be a student – a fact fully established for the first time in a slim volume issued today by Akros Publications under the title of *Early Lyrics by Hugh MacDiarmid*.

The editor to whose researches we owe the elucidation of the importance of the Ogilvie-MacDiarmid relationship, JK Annand, is himself a poet of individual accomplishment, whose collection of bairn-rhymes, *Sing it Aince for Pleisure*, is the most attractive book of poems about and for children since William Soutar's *Seeds in the Wind*.

Mr Annand also has the distinction of having recognised Hugh MacDiarmid's genius from the very first, at a period when his achievement aroused even fiercer controversy than it does today, its revolutionary revival of the authentic Scots tradition seeming far too radical even for many of the young.

Yet in 1926, when Mr Annand was only 18, he was already in correspondence with MacDiarmid about the latter's masterpiece, 'A Drunk Man Looks at the Thistle', before its publication later that year and he enjoyed the enviable privilege of being sent the great concluding sequence of the poem 'Yet Ha'e I Silence Left', in one of MacDiarmid's letters.

However, Mr Annand had one great advantage over most of his contemporaries, in that he too had been a pupil of George Ogilvie's and had had his eyes alerted to the emergence of novel creative talent.

As MacDiarmid himself says in the eloquent tribute especially written for the present volume, Ogilvie affected people, opening up perspective for them, indicating what he felt was the right direction in which they should develop.

'It was this, for instance, which resulted in Broughton producing a crop of writers, nearly all of whom in one way or another contributed to the revived use of Scots as a literary medium.

'They included Margaret Manson, Roderick Watson Kerr, Edward Albert, Albert Mackie, and JK Annand and there was no similarity of style among them – proof again that Ogilvie's influence stimulated individuality.'

If MacDiarmid is the father of modern Scottish poetry then Ogilvie deserves to be regarded as its grandfather, and Mr Annand, as a disciple and friend of both the writer and the teacher, is in the most strategic position to explain the relationship between them.

This he does chiefly through a penetrating investigation of the Grieve-Ogilvie correspondence, a fascinating sequence which begins in

1911, when the future poet was still in his teens, and continues until 1930, when his position as Scotland's greatest living makar was widely recognised, if still disputed.

While these letters show the continuing reliance which Grieve placed upon Ogilvie's opinion, and his continuing endeavour to ensure that it should be favourable, they also illuminate the different facets of the poet's developing career, from his first major impact upon the public as editor of the *Northern Numbers* anthology in 1920, up to the composition of 'A Drunk Man' and the critical reception of that major work.

The 'Drunk Man' letters alone make the present volume a bargain, for they make crystal clear both MacDiarmid's intention in the poem and his method of exemplifying it, thereby enhancing both the pleasure and the understanding of readers.

But as an additional delight the book also contains eight short poems from Grieve's letters to Ogilvie in 1921, seven of which have never before appeared in print, and all of which show him endeavouring to achieve that masterly brevity so notable in the Scots lyrics of 'Sangschaw' and 'Penny Wheep'.

These earlier efforts are in English, but in at least one of them 'In Memory', CM Grieve is well on the way towards becoming Hugh MacDiarmid.

> Only the rosebud I remember,
> Only the rosebud and the one green leaf
> – Beneath the grave-stone of the sky
> At last I lay them – a sufficient sheaf!

George Ogilvie (1871–1934). Principal Teacher of English, Broughton Junior Student Centre, later Broughton Higher Grade School 1904–1928.

> *Hugh MacDiarmid: Early Lyrics recently discovered among letters to his Schoolmaster and friend George Ogilvie, with an appreciation of George Ogilvie by Hugh MacDiarmid* edited with an introduction by JK Annand (Akros Publications 1968)
> *The Hugh MacDiarmid – George Ogilvie Letters*, edited by Catherine Kerrigan (Aberdeen University Press 1988)

8 June 1968

Apparently it is Poetry Week – at least, we are told so by a placard in the window of a Glasgow bookshop advertising the Phoenix Living Poets series.

Apart from that placard, however, there is no evidence that the Scottish public in general find poetry any more relevant during this particular week than in any other.

Yet three contemporary Scottish poets appear under the Phoenix imprint, and photographs of two of them feature in the bookshop window as part of the advertising display.

One photograph is a ludicrously unlikely likeness – Norman MacCaig looking like Rupert Brooke in a grey serge suit.

The other is all too appallingly accurate – Alan Bold like a belligerent bull glowering across a dyke.

In including both these poets in the same series, the Phoenix organisation shows itself as oscillating wildly between the sublime and the ridiculous.

MacCaig is widely regarded as the best of our poets writing in English, while many critics consider Bold to be among the worst.

The latter's Phoenix collection, *To Find the New*, displays both energy and ambition, but the energy is uncontrolled and the ambition of the vaulting kind which crumples in mid-air as a result of a faulty take-off.

A writer who suffers from a radically defective sense of rhythm cannot help but put down his feet in the wrong place, and Bold's work is forever stumbling over its own force and falling flat on its backside.

A commonplace intelligence and a blunt sensibility are also disadvantageous to a poet, and Bold possesses both disqualifications, making poem after poem excruciatingly bad, like McGonagall without even the relief of unconscious comedy.

It shows an oddly confused sense of values in the Phoenix publishers that they should push this unpromising apprentice while scarcely seeking to publicise the third Scottish poet on their list, that master-craftsman Sydney Tremayne.

Tremayne, who was born in Ayr in 1912 and published his first collection *Time and the Wind*, in 1948, is probably the most underestimated poet of his generation.

Perhaps his reputation has suffered from the fact that while he is a near contemporary of MacCaig and shares many of his attitudes, with a similar approach to his art and equal expertise, he has been a much less prolific writer – four volumes as against MacCaig's eight.

Such is the shortness of the public's memory that a poet who publishes at infrequent intervals is easily overlooked – and it is now six years since Phoenix issued Tremayne's last volume *The Swans of Berwick*.

Yet this is one of the most impressive and delightful verse collections of the past quarter-century, dazzlingly successful in its display of the poet's sensitive and seeking eye for significant detail, his impeccable ear for rhythm and verbal harmony, his scintillating intelligence, and the controlled tenderness of this sensibility.

His sonnet-like poem, 'The Fox', embodies all these qualities, with the animal at once itself and a symbol of suddenly remembered grief:

> A vision of silence startled me:
> A sinuous fox lightfooting past my door.
> Out of the corner of his yellow eye
> Glanced round his shoulder. Seeing nothing there,
> Skirted the tall dry biscuit coloured grass
> Unhurriedly, choosing the open way;
> Like an hallucination passed across
> To spring the trap forgotten many a day.
>
> One who was brave and frightened, fugitive,
> Fox coloured hair, eyes full of level flames,
> Leaps out of buried memory to live,
> The brightest thing in daylight. Swiftly comes
> The verbal thought how many years she's dead.
> The fox has slipped away in the dense wood.

The superb simplicity of those lines exemplifies the apparent artlessness which conceals superlative art. Tremayne has learned how to look and to listen, how to respond to touch and taste and scent, and how to organise the evidence of his senses into verse which is an illumination of experience. His wit is as flashingly acute as his passion is profoundly moving, and both are woven into poems which are at once masques and dances, sensuously vivid and rhythmically impelling.

Although Tremayne's work was overlooked by Scottish anthologisers until Norman MacCaig edited *Honour'd Shade* in 1959, and although he is still under-represented in subsequent anthologies, those of his poems which have appeared in *Scottish Poetry 1* (1966) and *Scottish Poetry 2* (1967) show that his current creations are even more concentratedly effective in their unity of intellect and emotion than those in *The Swans of Berwick*.

His next collection can scarcely avoid unanimous critical acclaim.

Norman MacCaig (1910–1996). Poet. He was generally recognised as one of Scotland's leading poets writing in English.
Collected Poems (New edition, Chatto and Windus 1990)

Alan Bold (1943–). Poet, critic, visual artist, literary biographer.
To Find the New (Phoenix Modern Poets 1968)

In This Corner: Selected Poems 1963–1983 (Macdonald 1983)
MacDiarmid: Christopher Murray Grieve: A Critical Biography (John Murray 1988)

Sydney Tremayne (1912–1986). Poet and journalist.
Time and the Wind (Collins 1948)
The Swans of Berwick (Chatto and Windus 1962)
Selected and New Poems (Chatto and Windus 1973)

15 June 1968

Although the title of JK Annand's new verse sequence, *Two Voices*, has been drawn from a famous sonnet by that eminent and eminently English poet Wordsworth, no writer has ever been more unmistakably Scottish than Annand, either in language or in attitude.

His literary Scots is close to the spoken tongue, and he writes it with the idiomatic ease of one who was born to the purple – in his case, the purple of the thistle. His irony, too, a blend of the grim and the gay, is as native to our poetical tradition as the chequered weave of the tartan.

His *Two Voices*, like Wordsworth's, are of the sea and the mountains, and a sequence which begins with the makar 'burd alane on a barren mountain tap' ends with his return from the perils of a war-time convoy in the Arctic when the 'sleep-hungry een o seamen' look across the Forth and find harbour in Edinburgh, 'speldered ablow the basalt cliffs and craigs, her birse o spires defiant in the air.'

In the mountain poems, where Annand is usually in holiday mood, the tone is generally light, reflecting his own light-heartedness in the enjoyment of climbing, 'wale o aa the manly sports,' although he gives expression to his ironical humour in a witty roll-call of the Lowland hills, making their names the basis of a folk-tale which is at once funny and fierce.

A graver note sounds through his poem on truth, where his glimpse of the Isles through the mists of a mountain-top is his vision of truth's suddenness in revelation and its equal speed in disappearance.

> Trith glents throu a slap
> In the dyke o Thocht
> As the Isles were to me
> In a sunblink brocht,
> When in Coire Mhic Fhearchair
> The mist broke a wee
> And they lay there like gowd
> In an emerant sea

> To be blottit frae sicht
> In the blink o an ee,
>
> And leave nocht but the mist
> And the bare rock, and me.

In those lines, Annand's style is as bare as the rock, and no less impressive in strength.

This strong simplicity is at least equally effective in his sea poems, which express a wider range of feeling from horror and grief to laughter and resolution, combining satire with pathos in 'What gart ye jine the navy, Jock?' and remorseless cruelty with the true lyric cry in 'Why bide ye by the sea, lassie?' – the latter an adaptation of the traditional ballad form to modern subject-matter in a poem which is both ferocious and fine.

But the sea has elements of beauty as well as brutality, and for these too Annand has the seeing eye –

> Sailin south to Iceland
> Out o the Arctic nicht
> We saw the snaw-capped mountains
> Alowe wi a rosy licht ...
> But here the lowe smooled yirdlins,
> Syne claucht the maintruck fast
> And a million starns were refleckit
> In the ice-encrustit mast.

The danger of using a style so unadorned as Annand's is that the poetry may crumble down into prose, and this disaster he is not always able to avoid, but usually he succeeds in combining simplicity with song.

This same combination is responsible for the success of his book of bairn rhymes, *Sing It Aince for Pleisure*, the best collection of children's verse in Scots for 30 years, now happily in its second edition.

While most of the pieces in this volume are specifically designed as rhyming entertainments for the young, and work admirably at that level, some penetrate considerably further into the life of things than most light verse can pierce, while others mingle comedy with criticism in a manner which has been traditionally Scottish since the beast fables of Robert Henryson in the fifteenth century.

When the stoat compares his fine new winter coat of white with the weasel's old brown one, the whitrick reads the other a lesson on the peril of pride which is grimly comic in its pointed brevity.

Said the whitrick to the stoat,
'I wadna mak owre muckle o't.
While nane will covet my auld coat
Your ermine fur wi tip o black
Will aiblins cleed a Provost's back.'

Both *Sing It Aince for Pleisure* and *Two Voices* are published by M Macdonald, Edinburgh, the printing-house whose director Calum Macdonald has been responsible for the issuing of more post-war poetry in Scots than all the established publishers together.

JK Annand (1908–1993). Poet, critic, editor and teacher. A former pupil of Broughton Higher Grade School, Edinburgh, where he followed in the footsteps of his friend CM Grieve (Hugh MacDiarmid) as editor of *The Broughton Magazine*, for which he reviewed 'Sangschaw' in 1925.
Sing It Aince For Pleisure (Macdonald 1965)
Two Voices (Macdonald 1968)
A Wale O Rhymes (Macdonald 1989)
Selected Poems 1925–1990 (The Mercat Press 1992)
Editor, *Lines Review* 1958–1959
Editor, *Lallans* 1973–1983

Calum Macdonald (1912–). Printer and publisher. The contribution that Macdonald has made to Scottish literature was recognised and celebrated when he was honoured with the major exhibition 'Calum Macdonald – Scottish Literary Publisher' at the National Library of Scotland in 1987.

13 July 1968

For more than 20 years there has been only one anthology of twentieth-century Scottish verse in the field, Maurice Lindsay's *Modern Scottish Poetry*, first published in 1946 and reissued, in an expanded edition, two years ago.

The merits of Mr Lindsay's selection of 'Scottish Renaissance' work are considerable, but its virtual monopoly has been unfortunate in a scene where tastes notoriously differ and a variety of views of the situation is greatly to be desired.

Until now, the reader seeking such variety has been obliged to consult the 'modern' sections of larger anthologies, surveying longer periods of Scottish poetry, Douglas Young's *Scottish Verse 1851–1951*, *The Oxford Book of Scottish Verse*, or the revised edition of the World's Classics *Book of Scottish Verse*, which came out only six month ago.

But there were drawbacks to all of these larger anthologies – Young's, which virtually ignores the distinction between verse and poetry, makes it extremely difficult for the reader to distinguish the pygmies from the giants.

The Oxford, on the other hand, has too much pro-Scots propaganda – some of it, I hasten to add, written by myself – and the World's Classics book, as revised by Maurice Lindsay, provides little more than a scaleddown (or in some cases, a scaled-up) version of his earlier view as presented in *Modern Scottish Poetry*.

Now, at long last, George Bruce presents a new and individual survey of Scottish poetry, since 1922, in *The Scottish Literary Revival* (Collier-Macmillan).

When the publishers contacted the poets who had been selected to appear in this anthology, they explained that it was primarily intended for the upper classes in secondary schools, but there is no mention of this fact in the book itself either on the dust-jacket or in the editor's helpful introduction.

In a volume of only 130 pages (including index), it is unfortunate that so much space has had to be given to the glossaries but perhaps in the circumstances the decision was inevitable – however much one may wish it could have been avoided.

Within the limited room at his disposal, the editor – whose own verse has been widely admired by his contemporaries and successors alike – has worked wonders, contriving to include no less than 38 poets in a 46-year period.

The oldest writer represented is the late and much-lamented Royal Limner for Scotland, Pittendrigh MacGillivray, whose name is a poem in itself. Born in 1856, MacGillivray lived on until the eve of the Second World War, dying only a year before the youngest contributor, Robin Fulton, was born in 1937.

Poets under the age of 30 are not included – on the whole, a wise decision in these days when more adolescent 'geniuses' than ever go up like rockets only to come down like sticks. In poetry, as in politics, more often than not it is wise to 'wait and see'.

The period with which Mr Bruce is concerned was dominated by the towering figure of Hugh MacDiarmid, whose stature as one of the greatest poets ever to write in Scots is now recognised everywhere, even in his native country, after a lifetime during which his work has received at least as much partial denigration as whole-hearted praise.

MacDiarmid's verse is so various in form and theme that it is virtually impossible to select from him, in a small anthology, a variety of poems which adequately reflects the range of his prodigious production, but the 13 poems Mr Bruce has chosen from different periods of his career make his genius unmistakeable.

While some critics have placed Edwin Muir's achievement on a level equal to MacDiarmid's, this I find myself unable to do. However, in many ways the work of this gentle mystic is complementary to that of the other's superb outgoing scope, and the 11 Muir poems presented here show every mode in which his reserved but distinguished talent expressed itself.

Among the younger poets, those who made their mark during or after the second war, Mr Bruce gives most space to Norman MacCaig (in English) and Sydney Goodsir Smith (in Scots), both of them writers of marked individuality and considerable range, whose work has had a discernible – sometimes all to discernible – influence on some of their successors.

In Gaelic, the only poets represented are Sorley Maclean and Derick Thomson, for whose work – even in translation – I have far too much respect to believe that the small selection included can do it justice. Here the limitations imposed upon Mr Bruce by the slight space at his disposal are more than usually evident.

If George Bruce's success is something less than entire, it is still remarkably large, and he deserves thanks and congratulations on his excellent endeavour to present a new generation of poetry readers with a novel interpretation of the modern Scottish scene.

Sorley Maclean (*Somhairle MacGill-Eain*) (1911–). One of Scotland's greatest Gaelic poets.
Dàin do Eimhir agus Dàin Eile (William Maclellan 1943)
O Choille gu Bearradh. (From Wood to Ridge). Collected Poems (Carcanet 1989)
Modern Scottish Poetry: An Anthology of the Scottish Renaissance 1920–1945, edited by Maurice Lindsay (Faber and Faber 1946, revised edition 1966). Second revised edition covers the period 1920–1985 (Robert Hale 1986).
Scottish Verse 1851–1951 edited by Douglas Young (Nelson 1952)
The Oxford Book of Scottish Verse edited by John MacQueen and Tom Scott (Clarendon Press 1966). Revised editions with corrections 1975 and 1981. Paperback edition 1989.
The Scottish Literary Revival – an anthology of twentieth-century poetry edited by George Bruce (Collier Macmillan 1968)
A Book Of Scottish Verse edited by Maurice Lindsay (World's Classics 1968)

20 July 1968

The best of Fred Urquhart's short stories are scarcely – if at all – inferior to the few superb examples of the art written by Lewis Grassic Gibbon in the early thirties, and they well deserve their recent republication in a collected edition from Rupert Hart-Davies issued in two volumes, *The Dying Stallion* (1967) and *The Ploughing Match* (1968).

Together with Mr Urquhart's first novel on adolescence in pre-war Edinburgh, *Time Will Knit* (1938), these tales show him to be the most distinguished of Gibbon's disciples, perhaps the only one whose work will bear comparison with his master's.

Even at that, however, the achievement is notably uneven, oscillating between a near approach to the perfect and close contact with the absurd.

Moreover, this unevenness occurs throughout the whole of Mr Urquhart's career, which spans three decades, from 'The Heretic', written in 1935, to 'Weep no More, My Lady', written in 1966.

'The Heretic', a study of the religious pressures brought to bear on an individual trapped by his own weaknesses and by the customs of a closed society, is a masterpiece etched in acid – whereas a story close to it in time, 'It Always Rains in Glasgow', written in 1938 about the Empire Exhibition, is as cornily 'coamic' as a script about the MacFlannels.

In the sixties again, 'Weep No More, My Lady', an attempt to combine the supernatural with the satirical, is too clumsily pedestrian to succeed, but the equally late 'Provide for Your Poor Sisters' paints a picture of the downfall of an Edinburgh spinster in colours which are at once horrifying and hilarious, sympathetic and savage.

In the first of these two volumes, *The Dying Stallion* – which is rather less impressive as a whole than the other – the best piece is probably the title story, in which a sudden disaster falling upon a great horse is presented not only naturalistically, but also symbolically, reflecting the powerlessness of the animal's ageing master to resist the views of the young.

In the second volume, 'The Ploughing Match', which gives its name to the book, is extremely fine in its contrasts between past and present in its presentation of the lack of understanding between different generations, and in its witness to the way in which the human mind can wrest a victory of sorts out of almost total defeat.

Fred Urquhart grew up in Edinburgh, and some of his best stories have their settings there or thereabouts, but during the war he worked on the land, and his tales of rural life are no less piercing in their penetration into the nature of things, no less revealing in the light they throw upon the Scottish character.

As far as range of characterisation is concerned, his most striking work is 'Once a Schoolmissy', set in a Scottish village and showing a number of schoolma'ams or former schoolma'ams, who have taught for some time in London, trying to deal with an entirely different environment.

This story, with its lesbian and other unladylike undertones, is a profound analysis of various kinds of failure and success and equally various attitudes towards them.

Although Mr Urquhart works within the comparatively narrow confines of the short story, his emotional scope is wide enough, and deep enough, to make room for an impressive expression of the complexities of human nature.

An English critic has recently praised these tales, which he calls 'proletarian studies,' for having 'opened the way for the playwrights of the last decade.'

But Mr Urquhart, the inheritor of Grassic Gibbon's mantle, deserves to be regarded as a significant creative artist in his own right rather than as some kind of Baptist figure to the rather dubious messiahs of the kitchen-sink school of drama.

He writes of the realities, the tragedies and the triumphs of ordinary life in a local setting, and his sympathetic insight and his unobtrusive skill resulted in the best of the localised stories becoming works of universal relevance.

These two volumes demonstrate once again that there is far more to be found in one's own parish than mere parochialism.

Fred Urquhart (1912–1995). Novelist and short story writer, he received a special award from the Scottish Arts Council only a few weeks before his death, for his contribution to Scottish literature.
Time Will Knit (Methuen 1938)
The Dying Stallion (Rupert Hart-Davies 1967)
The Ploughing Match (Rupert Hart-Davies 1968)
Proud Lady in a Cage (Paul Harris Publishing 1980)
Full Score: Short Stories, edited by Graeme Roberts (Aberdeen University Press 1989)

28 September 1968

'The brightest prospect that a Scotsman ever sees before him is the high road leading south to London' – whether we like it or not, there is still more than a grain of truth remaining in Dr Johnson's famous gibe, at least where cultural affairs are concerned.

In verse, the movement usually described as The Scottish Renaissance originated north of the Border, in little magazines edited by young CM Grieve in the days before he became Hugh MacDiarmid, but it took 20 years, and the issuing of a 'Renaissance' anthology by a London publisher, before the movement was accepted as being intellectually viable by that small section of the Scottish public which is interested in poetry.

'When London says turn, we all turn' – and when the English reviewers set the seal of their approval on MacDiarmid's *Collected Poems* at the appearance of that too-long-delayed volume for his 70th birthday six years ago, even those Anglo–Scottish journals which had denigrated or disregarded him for decades were constrained to turn Tuscan and give a strangled cheer.

If MacDiarmid had to wait until he was 70 to win over the London critics and their Anglo–Scottish imitators, this was largely because most of his very finest work is in Scots, a language towards which the English and their henchmen tend to react with hostility or suspicion.

Scottish poets writing in English whose work has chanced to coincide with fashionable London taste have had less time to wait before being praised in the English weeklies and consequently applauded in the Scottish dailies.

This happened to Edwin Muir in the forties, when the poems of legendary lore which he had been writing (regardless of fashion) for some 20 years happened to match a current English craze for myth-making. Ever since, there has been no lack of Scottish reviewers to laud Muir as a genius on account of some of his worst poems.

But if a fashionable London reputation may lead to a distorted view of a Scottish poet's achievement, at least it puts him on the map, it demonstrates his existence in the current artistic scene and thereby makes it impossible for Scottish newspaper criticism to continue to ignore him or present his work as merely negligible.

The latest Scottish beneficiary of this particular system – or lack of system – is Alan Jackson, who has published five volumes of verse in Scotland without ever gaining admission to the general anthologies of modern Scottish poetry but who now appears under the prestigious imprint of Penguin, accompanied by an Englishman and an American in *Penguin Modern Poets 12*.

My own admiration of Jackson's best work has been demonstrated in this column more than once, but I suspect that his adoption by Penguin is due less to the subtle sympathy and ironic wit of his most successful poems as to the raucous violence of others which shriek in concert with a fashionable taste for what the American poet Robert Lowell has called, 'raw, huge blood dripping goblets of unreasoned experience'.

Certainly this occasional violence – as much verbal as actual – is the main quality which Jackson shares with the other contributors to the current volume of Penguin verse, but his verse is at its weakest as poetry just where its violent rawness is most outspoken and outacted, and it would be a grave misfortune if he were to be misled by a passing acclaim into imagining that it is along such a channel that his true strength drives.

At only 28, Jackson has already achieved entirely individual attainment as a satirical symbolist, with such bitter brevities as 'Loss', which most tellingly reveals the all-too-frequent fate of beauty in a Scottish environment –

> A tulip fell deid
> bi ma doorstep the day
> dark rid the colour o blood
> wis the only yin come up this year
> A imagine it fell wi a thud

An unconventional stylist with a highly individual voice, Jackson shows a wide range of feeling and of form, moving from the epigrammatic wit of 'Young Politician' ('What a lovely, lovely moon. And it's in the constituency too') to the controlled passion of rage and sorrow in his picture of man as 'the worstest beast' and the sensuous richness and strangeness of a poem with the (to me) incomprehensible title of '3 l/g 4' which explores the mysteries of time and fate in terms of the superstitions of science and science-fiction.

Other verses, such as the shocking 'Fraulein' (rape followed by syphilis), may titillate teenagers at midnight poetry readings, but while frankness is an admirable virtue, it results only in sensationalism when presented, as here, in total isolation. Jackson is too good a poet to need to follow the passing craze.

Alan Jackson (1938–). Poet.
> *The Worstest Beast* (Kevin Press 1965)
> *Penguin Modern Poets* (Penguin 1968)
> *The Grim Wayfarer* (The Fulcrum Press 1969)
> *Salutations: Collected Poems 1960–1989* (Polygon 1990)

19 October 1968

Every poet is a haunted man, and among the ghosts that gibber behind him as he gropes his way through the maze of experience the most persistent has the shape of one of his early poems, a set of verses which happened to take the public fancy, was put into an anthology, and then into another, and then into the next, and the next ... until he feels the weight of those accumulated re-publications bowing down his shoulders with the unbearable pressure of monotonous immortality.

With WB Yeats the poems was 'The Lake Isle of Innisfree', with which he remained identified in the public mind for decades after he had passed on to other themes and different styles, so that it became one of his dearest desires to 'arise and go now' in any direction other than the one leading to the 'bee-loud glade'.

The process still goes on, and it still gives poets the shudders – as I learned the other day when consulting Stewart Conn about the choice of his work for a new anthology of contemporary Scottish verse.

Although Mr Conn is only in his early thirties, he has already become hag-ridden by The Ghost of Poetry Past to such an extent that it is a torment to him to open each successive Scottish anthology, for in every case the same creation of his own hand starts up out of the pages crying 'I am you and you are me and never the twain shall part!'

The poem is 'Todd', a subtle sympathetic tragi-comic sketch of Mr Conn's great-uncle, a countryman mad about horses who died.

> When the mechanised tractor came to pass.
> Now I think of him neighing to some saint
> In a simple heaven or, beyond complaint,
> Leaning across a fence and munching grass.

If Mr Conn happens to be reading this column, I have no doubt that at this point he has hurled the paper from him and rushed off screaming 'No, no, no, no, no! Not again! Not again!'

But of course he has only himself to blame, for 'Todd' evokes the identification between the hero and his horses with such superb simplicity, sensuousness and passion that no reader can resist it, and no anthology editor can forbear from including it in his choice.

My earliest acquaintance with the poem resulted from its publication in the first number of *Scottish Poetry* in 1966, and that same year it appeared again in Maurice Lindsay's *Scottish Renaissance* anthology for Faber, *Modern Scottish Poetry*.

This year, too, 'Todd' has been presented twice, in George Bruce's excellent selection, *The Scottish Literary Revival*, and in Mr Conn's own first full-length volume of verse, *Stoats in the Sunlight*, where it takes pride of place.

For this book Mr Conn has been given one of the Scottish Arts Council's new publication awards, a well-deserved tribute to a talent which it has been a pleasure to observe growing in range and resource over the years.

42

Perhaps the most remarkable of Mr Conn's gifts is his ability as a myth-maker, and in the first half of *Stoats* he gives a mythical quality, a universal relevance, to his memories of the Ayrshire farm where he spent much of his childhood and to the contrasts remorselessly wrought by time in the place and in the people who lived there.

> But acres crumple and the farm's new image
> Spreads over the old. As I face
> Its change a truck tips litter; hens assess
> Bright tins, then peck and squawk their rage.
> The truck spurts flame and I have no redress.

Here, as elsewhere, the myth-making is firmly rooted in reality, in the significant choice of details from everyday existence, which Mr Conn sees – and causes the reader to see through his command of visual images – as at once miraculous and mundane.

The second half of the book, where some of the myths employed are less personal and more literary, is not so consistently successful as the first, the verse tending to be overloaded with 'picturesque' imagery of a somewhat outdated romantic kind, but in at least two of his verse fables, 'Flight' and 'Ambush', poems which are at once contemporary and timeless, Mr Conn achieves a naked strength of style which at once matches and enhances the ruthlessness of his themes.

Equally ruthless, and yet with a tenderness all the more remarkable for its association with a refusal to avert the eyes from 'nature red in tooth and claw,' is his love poem 'The Fox in his Lair', with its starkly honest recognition of the common muck out of which all beauty springs.

> And you, my sweet,
> how can you hope
> to convince me
> you are all sweetness –
> when I know where
> your hands have burrowed?

In future anthologies there will be more of his poems to haunt Mr Conn in addition to 'Todd'.

Stewart Conn (1936–). Poet and playwright. Formerly Head of Drama BBC
   Radio Scotland.
   Thunder in the Air (Akros Publications 1967)
   The Chinese Tower (Macdonald 1967)
   Stoats in the Sunlight (Hutchison 1969)
   In the Kibble Palace: New and Selected Poems (Bloodaxe 1987)
   In the Blood (Bloodaxe 1995)

2 November 1968

Vital statistics are even more than usually vital to James Allan Ford.

As Registrar-General for Scotland, he is ultimately responsible for the accurate recording of our births, marriages and deaths, and as a novelist he finds such matters of at least equal concern. Strictly for the record, let it be registered that his latest novel, *A Judge of Men* (Hodder and Stoughton), has been honoured by a Scottish Arts Council publication award of £300.

This work is a very nice study in ambiguities, beginning with the title itself – but since the book is closely concerned with sex, perhaps it would more appropriate to refer to its *double entendres.*

Although the hero, Lord Falkland, a Senator of the College of Justice, is a judge by profession, and although he is characteristically Scottish in being by habit a somewhat censorious critic of his fellow-men, he is no judge of women – or at least, of the woman who is his wife.

The clue to the spring of tragedy which sets flowing the whole action of the book is to be found at the end of the penultimate chapter, in a snatch of conversation between two nurses officiating at Falkland's death-bed.

'Sex? He's dead against it.'

'Against it? Why did he marry a film star, then?'

This is the story of a winter of discontent in Edinburgh, but the judge's own personal discontent arises from the fact that his actress wife is a semi-invalid compelled to spend that season in Spain while he passes his working hours throughout the long bleak months in the still bleaker atmosphere of the criminal courts and returns in the evenings to a darkened, empty house without a glimmer of the understanding companionship he needs to keep his humanity warm.

Unable to get away for his usual winter holiday with his wife, Falkland gives vent to his frustration by denouncing sexual permissiveness from the bench while sentencing sexual offenders with all the rigour that the law permits.

As a result, he achieves notoriety in the press and receives two lots of anonymous letters on the general line that morality is a matter for private rather than public judgement and on the particular theme that his own wife's behaviour before marriage had scarcely been above reproach.

The first series of letters comes from an apprentice playwright, a young man in revolt who is also – to some extent – a revolting young man, convinced that Falkland represents the forces of 'power and death,' while the second series originates with a former lover of the judge's wife, an actor knocked off-balance by jealousy in a manner all too reminiscent of the judge's own loss of control as the result of enforced separation.

In the process, Falkland's dislike of permissiveness deepens into obsessions, and the end is a fatal stroke when he seems to discover that the allegations against his wife are true.

But, as recounted by Mr Ford, the novel is a great deal more subtle than the brief outline given above, for the psychological impulses behind the characters' actions are revealed – or rather, hinted at – only in the course of the plot's unfolding.

The mysteriousness of human motives is insisted upon as much by the book's construction, with its discovery, or part discovery, of one difference after another, as by the skilful and sympathetic characterisation of persons who are themselves by no means entirely sympathetic, although none of them is without some admirable qualities – except, perhaps, the former lover, a malicious and cowardly egotist.

With the judge, at once upright and obsessive, bound by firm standards and yet impelled by drives which are only partly conscious, the author has succeeded, despite formidable difficulty, in presenting a fine portrait in the round.

Again, his drawing of the self-centred young playwright, living partly in fantasy and partly in a desperate ambition to present the naked honesty of existence, is finely balanced.

The women – judge's wife, dramatist's mistress – are presented in less detail than the men, but their actions and reactions are persuasive throughout, and their greater fundamental endurance emerges convincingly.

Above all, Mr Ford has splendidly presented the environment in which his characters are compelled to function, winter Edinburgh.

If the book falls short of complete success, this is because the low disentangling of the characters' motives, however admirable in intention, results in much of the action remaining at least partly obscure until more than three-quarters of the space has been consumed.

But this is perhaps inevitable in the form Mr Ford has chosen, based on the 'who-dun-it.' The verdict, however, remains difficult to register – even for the Registrar-General for Scotland.

Murder most foul? Death by misadventure? Self-inflicted wounds? Each reader will reach his own decision.

James Allan Ford (1920–). Novelist. Registrar General for Scotland 1966–1969.

The Brave White Flag (Hodder and Stoughton 1961)
A Statue for a Public Place (Hodder and Stoughton 1965)
A Judge of Men (Hodder and Stoughton 1968)

14 December 1968

Buying someone a book as a Christmas gift is a chancy business, for nowhere do tastes differ more drastically than in the matter of literary likes and dislikes, and everyone's shelves must be littered with unread volumes bearing the inscription 'Merry Xmas'.

But there are exceptions to every rule, and for Christmas – or any other festive occasion – the most exceptional book I know is Robert Garioch's *Selected Poems*.

Garioch may not be the finest poet that modern Scotland has produced, but he is by far the funniest, with more belly-laughs per stanza than there are nips in a gill.

While his subject matter, present-day Edinburgh life, is as up to date as the introduction of an undressed female into a Festival discussion of the drama, his attitude is at least as old as the eighteenth century, since it exemplifies what a perceptive critic of Burns has described as 'the reductive idiom' – in other words, 'Caw the feet frae the High Heid-Yins'.

Although Garioch is a graduate of Edinburgh University, and used to be a schoolmaster, he identifies neither with the professional class nor with the bourgeoisie, but presents himself as a 'drop-out,' wearing 'siven-and-saxpenny flannen breeches,' speaking dialect, writing in the language of the pub, and preferring the company of drouthy drinkers to the acquaintance of the 'unco guid'.

The underdog who bites the ankles of the powerful and the pretentious is, in various sizes, shapes and forms, the truly dominant character in most of the highly hilarious contributions to his series of *Sixteen Edinburgh Sonnets*.

In 'Glisk of the Great', a famous singer, fat and flushed with wine, cracks doubtful jokes with a trio of 'notorious bailies' as they sally forth from the NB Grill and sail away in a municipal Rolls-Royce, followed by an unprivileged on-looker's sardonic comment –

> Nou that's the kinna thing I like to see;
> tho ye and I look on and canna jyne in,
> it gies our toun some tone, ye'll aa agree.

In 'Queer Ongauns', the official mace is dismissively described as 'a muckle siller cosh', and the incomprehensible activities of the office-bearers who accompany it are sternly denounced by the unsophisticated spectator – 'shame on them aa, whatever they were daean!'

In 'Heard in the Cougate', a reception arranged for 'The King o Norway wi his royal suite' is reduced to absurdity by being discussed in gutter-Scots liberally interspersed with gobs of spit – 'wi aw thae, hechyeuch! fforeign po'entates'.

Even in 'Elegy', where Garioch appears in person, as a 'new-cleckit dominie', he represents himself as biting the hands that fed him inadequate fodder, the headmasters who criticised his aptitude and his appearance and his inability to live on his salary –'Weill, gin they arena deid, it's time they were'.

In 'Did Ye See Me?' where Garioch gives a unique performance clad in complete academic regalia, he blows up the bubble of professional pomposity by means of a ludicrously persistent employment of archaistic rhymes, and then pricks it with the pin of illiterate ribaldry.

> I'll tell ye of ane great occasioun:
> I took part in in a graund receptioun ...
> the hale ploy was my ain conceptioun;
> I was asked to gie a dissertatioun.
>
> The functioun was held in the aipen air,
> a peety, that; the keelies of the toun,
> a toozie lot, gat word of the affair.
>
> We cudnae stopt it: they jist gaithert roun
> To mak sarcastic cracks and grin and stare,
> I wisht I hadnae worn my M.A. goun.

Both masterly and merciless, that poem is not the only one in which Garioch is ferociously funny at the expense of himself and other Arts graduates. In the whole of contemporary Scottish poetry, there is nothing more amusing, or more appalling, than his picture of the awful fate of the Edinburgh MA condemned to a life-sentence of school-mastering 'without the option'.

> Sae ilka week and month and year
> his life is tined in endless steir,
> grindan awa in second-gear gin teaching be his fate ...
> Lat onie young poetic chiel
> that reads thae lines tak tent richt weill:
> THINK TWICE, OR IT'S OWRE LATE!

Garioch's comic contempt for his own profession, the poorest-paid and the least-privileged in the land, has led him to identify himself with the underpaid and the underprivileged in general, and to write the most devastating satires of our contemporary cash-culture in post-war Scots verse.

Robert Garioch (1909–1981). Poet.
> *Selected Poems* with an introduction by Sydney Goodsir Smith (Macdonald 1966)
> *Docktor Faust in Rose Street* (Macdonald 1973)
> *Robert Garioch – Complete Poetical Works* edited by Robin Fulton (Macdonald 1983)

26 April 1969

'All men are equal,' declared the revolutionaries in George Orwell's *Animal Farm* – but once they had seized power and established themselves in control, they were quick to add the rider that 'some are more equal than others'. One doesn't need to be an exponent of Orwellian irony to come to the conclusion that, so far as poets are concerned, the exact opposite is true, and that 'All poets are unequal, but some are more unequal than others'.

In the latter category Maurice Lindsay, whose new collection *This Business of Living* (Akros Publications) looses some lame ducks among its soaring larks, is by no means least.

Too often, Mr Lindsay spoils the simple adequacy of a descriptive poem by trying to evaluate it into intellectual significance by means of a moralistic conclusion which is too trite to be felt as true. Equally frequently, when attempting to interpret experience in philosophical terms throughout a poem's course, he gasps and flounders like a fish out of water.

In such passages, too, his style tends to slacken, to lose rhythmical urgency and dexterity, while his characteristic trick of juggling with parts of speech – elsewhere often employed with such skilful sleight-of-hand that the reader is scarcely aware of the means whereby the powerful impact he creates has achieved its end – becomes clumsy and unconvincing.

But when Mr Lindsay is on form and in such complete control that description and action are left to speak for themselves, he produces work which is brilliantly successful at every level, technically, emotionally and intellectually.

His senses are vividly alive to the sights and sounds and scents of the natural world, and when he refrains from trying to tease them into patterns of metaphysical explanation, he is able to allow his enviable gift for seizing upon essential details to create a design which is itself a sufficient interpretation of the experience which the poem enshrines – as in the lyrical loveliness of 'Stones in Sky and Water'.

The synthesis of beauty and cruelty, ruthlessness and pity, action and thought and feeling in 'At the Mouth of the Ardyne' is expressed with such perfectly controlled economy, that the poem is into the heart like a honed dagger through the ribs before the reader realises that the point has struck.

> The water rubs against itself,
> glancing many faces at me.
> One winces as the dropped fly
> tears its tension. Then it heals ...
>
> Then a scar opens.
> Something of water is ripped out,
> a struggle with swung air.
> I batter it on a loaf of stone.
>
> The water turns passing faces,
> innumerable pieces of silver.
> I wash my hands, pack up, and
> go home wishing I hadn't come.
>
> Later, I eat my guilt.

That poem is as penetratingly perceptive about human nature as about the natural world in which it operates, and the best pieces in *This Business of Living* show a widening and a deepening of Mr Lindsay's range to encompass the ambiguities of art and love in 'A Ballad of Orpheus' and the brutal defeat of love by hatred, in 'Glasgow Nocturne', which demonstrates that his talent is still developing, still discovering novel themes in the world around it and new ways of expressing them through its own capacity for successful experiment.

In addition to his delectable gifts as a poet, Mr Lindsay has also performed much valuable work as editor, with the *Poetry Scotland* collections during the war, with the Faber *Modern Scottish Poetry* anthologies in 1946 and 1966, with the contemporary *Scottish Poetry* annuals and with the selected poems of such different writers as John Davidson and Sir David Lindsay, author of the only pre-Reformation dramatic masterpiece to have survived in Scotland, *Ane Satyre of the Thrie Estaits*.

Although Sir Tyrone Guthrie's production of this gorgeous gallimaufry of comedy, tragedy, farce, irony, wit, lyricism and immorally moral didacticism was produced three times at the Edinburgh Festival in the forties and fifties, it is now ten years since the last revival.

The new production which opens in the Bute Hall of Glasgow Unversity on April 26 and runs for the following week should come as a revelation to all who have never seen the work before, and as a confirmation of its inexhaustible energy to all who have already experienced its unmatched drive and invention.

Maurice Lindsay (1918–). Poet, literary historian, broadcaster; formerly Programme Controller, Border Television; Director, Scottish Civic Trust 1967–1983.

This Business of Living (Akros Publications 1969)

Selected Poems 1942–1972 (Robert Hale 1973)

A History of Scottish Literature (Robert Hale 1977; revised paperback edition 1992)

Collected Poems 1940–1990 (Aberdeen University Press 1990)

News of the World – Last Poems (Scottish Cultural Press 1995)

3 May 1969

'The most prolific, the most passionate and the most powerful of that generation of poets writing in Scots – the so-called Lallans makars – who published their first collections during or just after the last war.'

That description of Sydney Goodsir Smith is drawn from one of the three articles on his work in the new number of the magazine *Akros*, and the writer is the author of this column, who first went on record as an admirer of Goodsir Smith's poetry as early as 1946, before the latter had published the verse which has won him critical recognition as the greatest love poet in Scots since Burns.

Now, in another of the *Akros* articles, no less a figure than Hugh MacDiarmid, the father of twentieth century Scottish poetry, writes of Goodsir Smith that 'he insofar as that is possible at all, is the Burns *de nos jours*'.

Yet there is scarcely more chance of the Burns Federation appointing Goodsir Smith as its 'Rab Reincarnated' than there is of the present Secretary of State for Scotland recommending Hugh MacDiarmid for the place in the Order of Merit which has been vacant since the death of TS Eliot.

For while Goodsir Smith and MacDiarmid resemble Burns in their rebellion against the social order, they differ from him in that authority has been unable to stifle their protests.

Moreover, Goodsir Smith has savaged the Burns Federation with his scorn for their disregard of every Scottish poet except 'The Bard of

Immortal Mummery' – and even if the Federation would prefer to forget the vehemence of his views, *Akros* reminds them by reprinting his attack in its current editorial.

Besides, as MacDiarmid points out, Goodsir Smith's 'Scots usages are … embedded in contexts that have little in common with what is commonly regarded as the Burns tradition and are embellished with a range of reference that is *caviare to the general.*'

Yet, even if the Federation prefers haggis to caviare, it remains true – as MacDiarmid also observes – that 'the burden of all Sydney's poetry is similar to that of Burns', with sexual love as its main theme and with 'elements of social protest, radical politics, a contempt for the unco guid'.

All of these aspects of Goodsir Smith's talent are reflected in one or other of the nine poems which he contributes to *Akros*. A representative selection of his most recent work, these range from the cutting anti-political contempt of 'Three Men Make a Revolution', where the title is an ironical quotation from Lenin, to the carefree celebration of the wine of the country in 'Tak Aff Your Dram', where the title derives from Burns without any irony whatever, and to the naked passion of 'The Kenless Strand', which springs directly out of individual experience of love.

While much of his most powerful love poetry is expressed in terms of personal lyricism, he is equally effective in the narrative and dramatic forms of 'Under the Eildon Tree', a sequence of 24 'elegies', the subject of an *Akros* article by Robert Garioch, who blends admiration with analysis in a nice demonstration of sympathetic skill.

Whether the influence of Goodsir Smith's work can be traced in the verse of the eight other writers who contribute poems in Scots to the current *Akros* it is not for me to say, since I am one of them, but the variety of subject-matter and of style in these contributions would seem to show that the Scots tradition, which has been 'an unconscionable time a-dying', will continue yet awhile to defy the prophets who prognosticate its imminent end.

It says much for the open-mindedness of this magazine's editor, Duncan Glen, that one of these poems, 'No Stolgie for Ben Dorain', by Tom Scott, is an attack on the finest features of the previous issue, Iain Crichton Smith's decorous translation of Duncan Ban Macintyre's eighteenth century Gaelic masterpiece, *Ben Dorain*.

Also in that previous issue, Alastair Mackie expressed the view that Rimbaud's *Bateau Ivre* was scarcely suitable for translation into Scots – and in the present number Mr Glen gives Mr Mackie the opportunity to prove or disprove that view in a Scots version of the French original called 'The Drucken Boat'.

While one may have one's doubts about the result, Mr Mackie deserves as much credit for making the attempt as was given to Edwin Morgan for his Scots translation of Mayokovsky's Russian poem on Brooklyn Bridge, published in the last issue.

Mr Morgan is one of eight Scottish writers given a £300 publications award by the Scottish Arts Council for recent work, and in offering him our congratulations we also commend to readers the splendid collection of poems for which his award was made, *The Second Life*.

Sydney Goodsir Smith (1915–1975). Poet, critic, editor and artist.
 The Deevil's Waltz (William Maclellan 1946)
 Under The Eildon Tree – A Poem in XXIV elegies (Serif Books 1948, second revised edition 1954)
 Figs and Thistles (Oliver and Boyd 1959)
 Collected Poems 1941–1975 (John Calder 1975)
 Editor, *Lines Review* 1954–1957

Alastair Mackie (1925–1995). Poet and teacher.
 Clytach (Akros Publications 1972)
 At the Heich Kirk-yaird (Akros Publications 1974)
 Backgreen Odyssey and Ither Poems (Rainbow Books 1980)
 Ingaitherins: Selected Poems (Aberdeen University Press 1987)

10 May 1969

The ironies of literary life in Scotland never cease to delight me and I was particularly pleased when the President of the 1320 Club, Hugh MacDiarmid, invited me to read my verse at a series of poetry recitals which the Club is organising for the next Edinburgh Festival, because on the same day that I received that invitation I opened the new number of the Club's quarterly, *Catalyst*, to find myself denounced in a 'letter to the editor' which bears all the marks of being a fabrication.

The editor of *Catalyst*, a Mr William Neill, would to do well to recall Noel Coward's words to another literary apprentice – 'If you can't take criticism, get out of this business'.

There is plenty to criticise on the arts side of the current *Catalyst,* although less than there is to praise, for most of the poems are of remarkable quality. A patriotic ode, 'Rebukes', by George Campbell Hay, is so effectively controlled in its sensuous passion, even when read only in its English prose translation, that the Gaelic original must be magnificent.

Alan Bold's 'In a Second-hand City Bookshop' is far and away the best poem by this writer that I have ever seen, the warmth of its human sympathy beautifully tempered by witty intelligence, the simplicity of the style matched by a clear flow of movement.

In 'Jay', Tom Scott is at the peak of his satirical form, in a savagely comic attack on a brother bard (if he will forgive the phrase) rendered all the more scathingly successful for being a stylistic parody of the victim's own manner.

The articles on the arts, however, are at the other extreme from the effective verse, consisting of a piece on folksong which is both disjointed and pedestrian, and a review of the first two volumes in the *Modern Scottish Poets* series published by Caithness Books where the reviewer makes the fatal error of quoting lines of nearly illiterate Lallans and praising them as if they were perfection.

It does no good to the Scottish literary movement to applaud mediocre work as if it were masterly, for that is a self-defeating process which achieves no more than providing opportunities for the movement's adverse critics to dismiss the whole endeavour as havers.

A case in point occurs in the current issue of *Scottish International* where Alan Jackson, reviewing these same Caithness Books of verse, seizes upon the chance given him by Duncan Glen in a far too flattering introduction to David Morrison's prentice poems, and attacks what he calls 'a political and dogmatic blind spot, concerning Lallans, which accepts bad work ... because it fits into the programme'.

From this particular stabbing stroke Mr Jackson proceeds to general assassination, with the remark that, 'There is undoubtedly some peculiar Scottish sickness at work here; and it has allowed several other writers to make reputations by turning their paranoia into illiteracy'.

On that my own comment, from the viewpoint of one of the comparatively few Scottish poets who writes both in Scots and in English, would be that there is yet another peculiar Scottish sickness, which has allowed several younger Scottish writers to make their reputations by refusing to see any merit at all in any Lallans poems whatsoever.

Apart from the snide remarks quoted above, I find Mr Jackson's review only too true in its analysis of the incompetence of the Caithness Books poets, and I applaud his courage in refusing to play the grand old Caledonian caper of 'you scratch my book and I'll scratch yours'.

This number of *Scottish International* is a marked improvement on its immediate predecessor, giving far more space to the discussion of creative work in Scotland and to the presentation of examples in pictorial art in fiction and in verse.

Two articles are particularly brilliant, John Purser's on the radio operas commissioned by the 'Scottish' BBC, and Hamish Henderson's on and around Hugh MacDiarmid's prose selection, *The Uncanny Scot,* a review which is scarcely less informed or less fantastically funny, than the book itself.

The three short stories, by a trio of literary ladies, have too much whimsy for my own no doubt brutalised masculine taste, but none is without merit, and the folk tale recited by Bella Higgins has an odd pointless charm.

For the poetry, the names of Robin Fulton, Sydney Tremayne, Iain Crichton Smith and Edwin Morgan are themselves sufficient guarantee of quality. But the articles on John and Robert Kennedy, Norman Mailer and Tenessee Williams, however well written – and the last is not – seem to me a waste of space, re-hashing topics which have been done to death in countless publications all over the place.

On the other hand, Arthur Marwick's briefly witty attack on the quality of Scottish life, 'A Plea for Free Movement', while deliberately designed to send dedicated nationalists into a frenzy, has all the appeal of freshness.

A stimulating issue, considered as a whole.

William Neill (1922–). Tri-lingual poet in Scots, Gaelic and English.
Selected Poems 1969–1992 (Canongate 1994)
Editor, *Catalyst* 1968–1970
Editor, *Lallans* 1984–1987

George Campbell Hay (*Deòrsa Mac Iain Deòrsa)* (1915–1984). Son of the novelist J MacDougall Hay, poet in Gaelic, English and Scots.
Wind on Loch Fyne (Oliver and Boyd 1948)
Fuaran Sléiph (William Maclellan 1948)
Seeker Reaper with an introduction by Angus Martin and illustrations by Archie MacAlister (Saltire Society 1988)

David Morrison (1942–). Poet, editor and librarian.
The White Hind and Other Poems, with an introduction by Duncan Glen (Caithness Books 1968)
The Constant Tide: Selected Poems (Pulteney Press 1986)
The Cutting Edge: Collected Poems (forthcoming, Scottish Cultural Press 1997)
Editor, *Scotia Review* 1972–1978

John Purser (1942–). Composer, musicologist, and lecturer; poet, playwright and broadcaster.
The Counting Stick (Aquila 1976)
A Shore of the Wind (Aquila 1980)
Scotland's Music – A History of the Traditional and Classical Music of Scotland from Early Times to the Present Day (Mainstream 1992)

31 May 1969

Burns once remarked that the poet who knows his business will reserve his most effective matter for 'a concluding stroke,' ending his poem on a peak instead of at the foot of a precipice, and if this observation applies to poets themselves it is equally applicable to editors of poetry, who demonstrate their knowledge of their business by ascertaining that any selection of verse which they may make will end at least as strongly as it began.

As a poet himself, and as an experienced editor, George Bruce knows his business twice times over, and the disc of selected Scottish verse which he has chosen, *The Scottish Renaissance: Poems 1922–1966*, begins with the greatest of our twentieth century makars, Hugh MacDiarmid, and ends with the most versatile – and not the least vivid – of our younger writers, Iain Crichton Smith.

It ends, too, with lines which are nicely apposite to the record as a whole, the last lines of Crichton Smith's 'Two Girls Singing':

> And it wasn't the words or tune. It was the singing,
> It was the human sweetness
> … the unpredicted voices of our kind.

The actual voices on the disc belong to two of our finest poetry readers, Tom Fleming and Bryden Murdoch.

Such is their skill and sympathy that they give tongue to the individual timbre of every poet whose work finds vocal expression in 'the human sweetness' which they add to the written word.

This is no slight achievement, for represented on the record are no less than 13 modern Scottish poets, chosen by Mr Bruce from the 38 who were included in his anthology *The Scottish Literary Revival*, published by Collier-Macmillan last year.

Quite apart from the fact that it contains my own poem 'Haar in Princes Street', this record is as remarkable for its width of range as for its delicacy of judgement and includes examples of the finest work of all the various 'schools' of twentieth century Scottish poetry, from MacDiarmid's revitalisation of Scots as a language for universal themes, in the early twenties, to the use of a kind of English suited to the expression of Scottish themes in the early sixties.

Poetry is, above all, a spoken art – a fact which our enslavement to the written word has caused too many of the public, and even some of the poets themselves, to forget too often.

This record will remind them that the sound of poems is an integral element in their effect, that they are created in order to be spoken by 'the unpredicted voices of our kind'.

Without 'the human sweetness' of the voice, poetry lacks an essential dimension, a resonance and reverberation for which print is no substitute.

Opportunities for hearing Scottish poetry superbly spoken are all too few, but thanks to Douglas Gray, the 'onelie begetter' of the Scottish Records company which has produced the present disc, when they do occur they are well worth lending an ear. Should a sequel to this record ever appear, it will have to go on from Crichton Smith (born 1928) to Tom Buchan (born 1931), who has just published his first collection of verse *Dolphins at Cochin* (Barrie and Rockliff).

One of Mr Buchan's most effective poems, a fine fusion of sensuous affirmation and intellectual questioning, is called 'Doubting Thomas', and his starting-point as a writer is from a position of disenchantment so extreme as to be almost total.

Sometimes, indeed, he gets stuck on this start and stays there running on the spot of facile cynicism but when passion impels him forward his progress is all the more impressive for having to be struggled for against the restraints of disillusion.

The wry comedy of 'Scotland the Wee', a satire on this 'land of the millionaire draper, whisky vomit and the Hillman Imp' which is briefly etched in acid, with a sting in every phrase, modulates into the ironic self-criticism of 'The Weekend Naturalist,' where he combines a MacCaigish appreciation of the Highland scene with a keenly individual realisation of his own imperfections as an explorer of that scene-in-itself.

Mr Buchan's range of theme and subject matter is wide, from the imaginative limitations of astronauts to the emotional emptiness of a Scottish beach, but always an essential integrity of approach enables him to avoid the slightest suspicion of an inflated style and to write with a stark precision which nevertheless strikes upon the *mot juste* to telling effect.

For while Mr Buchan is a highly intelligent writer, he is well aware that man cannot live by the mind alone, and his philosophical speculations seldom lose touch with sensuous experience: 'One needs the shepherd boy unwashed on his yellow hill and the fierce sunlight drawing music from his bitter pipe'.

Tom Buchan (1931–1995). Poet, editor and playwright.
Dolphins at Cochin (Barrie and Rockliff 1969)
Poems 1969–1972 (The Poni Press 1972)
Editor, *Scottish International* 1973–1974

14 June 1969

Writing a 25-page article on 'Scottish Poetry in 1968' for the American academic review *Studies in Scottish Literature*, I was obliged to discuss no less than 15 individual collections of verse, three poetry magazines and two anthologies, all produced within a single twelvemonth, and it occurs to me that the prime source of all this activity by so many poets and editors and publishers was one man.

Hugh MacDiarmid, of course.

He, more than any other single individual, has been responsible for the revolution in Scottish poetry which has taken place in the fifty years since the end of the First World War.

At the beginning of this century, when Professor JH Millar published his *Literary History of Scotland*, it seemed to him that the Scottish literary tradition had at last given up the ghost – 'Its resources as regards verse,' he wrote, 'appear to be exhausted, and all its conventions worn to a thread'.

But in 1969, Scottish literature proves to have confounded the prophets by flourishing like the green bay tree. For when Millar sang his swansong over Scots verse in 1903, he had sufficient wit and wisdom to add these final words: 'Genius indeed, is another matter. For genius no man can be answerable. Its ways are not our ways; its spirit bloweth where it listeth; and no "system of national education", however well-advised in theory or servicable in practice, can do anything to affect its production or much to affect its development.'

The genius to whom Millar unwittingly referred was young Chris Grieve, then 11 years old, who emerged from a 'system of national education' teaching little Scots and less Scottish literature to become Hugh MacDiarmid, one of the very greatest poets in the Scots tradition.

During the twenties and thirties, the question of MacDiarmid's achievement was highly controversial – and still more so the work of those writers whom he associated with himself in the movement he called 'The Scottish Renaissance'.

But in 1946, 20 years after the publication of MacDiarmid's masterpiece, *A Drunk Man Looks at the Thistle*, he and his disciples achieved critical respectability when Messrs Faber and Faber of London, whose poetry list rejoiced in the personal supervision of the venerable TS Eliot, issued *Modern Scottish Poetry: An Anthology of the Scottish Renaissance*.

Since then there has been such a complete reversal of the status of contemporary Scottish poetry that whereas in 1946 questions on MacDiarmid were conspicuous by their absence even from final

Honours papers in English at the universities, in 1969 they are equally conspicuous by their presence even in papers for the SCE in our schools.

The prestige which MacDiarmid was the first twentieth century Scottish writer to achieve in the extra-academic world not only won a university place for the Michty Makar himself, but also opened the door for such other contemporaries as Muir, Bridie, Grassic Gibbon, Soutar and Gunn.

Moreover, the realisation – or even, at worst the mere admission – that Scottish literature, as a distinct and distinctive entity, is still alive and developing in the twentieth century has had a powerful effect in stimulating the study of that literature in earlier periods.

No longer does that study languish in the no doubt honourable but nonetheless neglected category of a dead discipline, but on the contrary it is regarded by scholars and students alike, as an essential part of a still continuing process in the light of which there is equally continuing modification of attitudes to work of every period of the past.

All of this I was reminded of while watching the 15-minute film on MacDiarmid's life and work produced by Douglas Gray for Educational Films of Scotland.

Called simply – and sufficiently – *MacDiarmid*, this counter-points a conversation with the poet in his present home outside Biggar in Lanarkshire against scenes shot in his native Langholm in Dumfriesshire and some of the justly-famous poems – 'Crowdieknowe', 'At My Father's Grave', 'Drums in the Walligate' – which emerged from his formative years in that stimulating environment.

A film which is illuminating both visually and intellectually, *MacDiarmid* should be shown in all our schools and universities as an introduction to the genius who has given us a twentieth century Scottish poetry in which to take the highest pride.

I wish I believed it would be. But so many of our educationists are still so conscious of their ignorance of all things Scottish and so parochially determined to avoid the slightest suspicion of parochialism, that it is difficult to be optimistic on such a point.

John Hepburn Millar (1864–1929). Professor of Constitutional Law, University of Edinburgh 1909–1925.

A Literary History of Scotland (T Fisher Unwin 1903) For many years the standard work on Scottish literature; contains one of the first attacks on the late-nineteenth-century 'Kailyard' novelists.

12 July 1969

On the appearance of the first two volumes in the Modern Scottish Poets series published by Caithness Books, this column welcomed the project and commended the initiative of the publisher, John Humphries.

At the same time, however, it was necessary to express regret that Mr Humphries had begun by issuing the work of a pair of such comparatively undistinguished poets as David Morrison and Charles Senior and to point out that the series would have made much more initial impact if it had started with books by Robin Fulton and Ronald Eadie Munro, who were scheduled to appear third and fourth.

One result of that article was a 'letter to the Editor' from Mr Humphries in which he defended his choice of Messrs Morrison and Senior on grounds which had little or no relevance to their literary merit (or lack of it).

Another result was that when the third volume in the series, *Inventories*, by Robin Fulton, appeared in May, a review copy failed to reach the *Scots Independent,* and it was only by chance that we came to learn of its publication.

Since then, however, we have been fortunate enough to come into possession of a copy in which a variety of printing errors have been corrected by the poet's own fair hand, so that our views, however belatedly expressed, have the virtue of being based on a more accurate text of the poems than might otherwise have been the case.

Inventories appears only some 18 months after Mr Fulton's previous collection, *Instances* (Macdonald, Edinburgh, 1967), and all of its 43 poems have been written in a period of not much more than a year, from August 1967 to December 1968.

This means that Time, which is not only a great healer but a great winnower too, has not had any considerable opportunity to get to work at the essential process of persuading the author that some of his poems are less successful than others and might merit revision – or even, in some cases, complete suppression.

As a result, *Inventories* is marred by the inclusion of a number of pieces where ideas have failed to ignite when rubbed together. Or where emotions with insufficient impetus to maintain their flight fall into spinning nosedives. Or where techniques are not quite dazzling enough to avoid betraying the tricks behind their expertise.

But even after its not infrequent failures have been discarded, *Inventories* remains an impressive volume, distinguishing its author – who is still only 32 – as the most variously talented poet of his generation.

No less than six poems from this collection have been chosen by Norman MacCaig and myself for an anthology of *Contemporary Scottish Poetry 1959–1969* which is to be published shortly, and if space had permitted we should have had no difficulty in doubling that choice, for Mr Fulton's wide range of themes is matched by the most delicately focused intensity of vision.

An admirable conciseness enables him to express his insights in the minimum of space and yet with no sacrifice either of clarity or of passion.

As in 'How to Survive', which contrasts the appearance of a waterdrop to the naked eye with its magnified revelation as 'a vast world of interrelated life' –

> consider fortunate Noah
> one thing he might have taken
> along with his stud menagerie
> was a specimen waterdrop
> to demonstrate the true nature
> of the murderous element he rode

His keen sighted appreciation of the significant details of the Scottish landscape issues in entirely individual poems where appearances become symbols of emotional and intellectual experiences, as in 'A Discovery', a love poem which moves out from personal passion to embrace the whole world of being, and in 'Remote', where the apparent liberty of escape into the natural scene is counterpointed with the impossibility of leaving one's prepossessions behind.

In 'A Meticulous Observer', he transforms his awareness of his own weaknesses into a source of strength, and in 'Attic Finds' he finds a telling image for the transitoriness of beauty which is as finely original as it is illuminating; while 'Clearing Up' expresses the strangeness of the familiar self with a seeming simplicity which nevertheless penetrates to the inner depth of the personality.

If Mr Fulton both writes and publishes too much, this is a fault on the right side, for the young poet who isn't fecund is less likely to develop his talent than one who finds occasions for poetry anywhere and everywhere.

One of the most striking poems in this book is called 'A Man with a Lucky Gift'. It isn't a self-portrait, but the title could and should be applied to the writer too.

Charles Senior (1918–1975). Poet and bookseller.
Selected Poems (Macdonald 1966)
Harbingers (Caithness Books 1968)

Robin Fulton (1937–). Poet, critic and translator. Editor, *Lines Review*, 1967–1977.

Inventories (Caithness Books 1969)

Selected Poems 1963-1978 (Macdonald 1980)

Contemporary Scottish Verse 1959–1969 edited by Norman MacCaig and Alexander Scott (Calder and Boyars 1970)

4 October 1969

'It should go without saying that the essential subject-matter of the literature of a small nation in a state of rebirth will be the life of that nation.'

With those challenging words, John Herdman nails his saltire colours to the literary mast in a trenchant article on 'Literature and National Self-Confidence' published in the autumn issue of the 1320 Club's quarterly, *Catalyst*.

On the face of it, his statement seems to be one with which anybody and everybody concerned with the survival and revival of Scottish nationhood is bound to agree. Yet, when considered more closely, Mr Herdman's striking sentence can be seen to beg as many questions as it contains subordinate clauses.

What is the meaning of the phrase *essential subject matter*? Who decides that a small nation is or is not in a state of rebirth, the politicians or the poets and prose-writers?

And how widely, or how narrowly, is the *scope of the life of that nation* to be interpreted?

Literary works are not composed by nations as such, big or small, but by individual writers whose *essential subject-matter* is bound to vary in accordance with their differing interests.

Authors will inevitably differ, too, in their opinions of whether a condition of national rebirth actually does exist – the classic example of this, to which Mr Herdman refers indirectly, is the diametrical opposition of views between Hugh MacDiarmid and Lewis Grassic Gibbon in *Scottish Scene*, the book where they 'co-operated' to present two radically contrasted pictures of Scotland in the early thirties.

In dealing with the life of any nation, some writers will prefer to concentrate most of their attention on indigenous aspects, but others will be more concerned with the relationships between their own particular society and various elements of the world around it.

All of this is a question of emphasis, a matter of personal preference, and any critic who suggests that writers should be expected to follow one particular approach and one only is imposing a restriction which every author is bound to regard as intolerable.

I say this all the more strongly because this same issue of *Catalyst* contains, on the page facing Mr Herdman's stimulating article, a poem of my own which is very closely concerned with Scottish life – and death – 'Dear Isle', which attempts to express the tragic emptiness of contemporary Mull.

That this kind of subject matter is more *essential* to present day Scottish literature than a concern with space travel or Oriental resistance movements or the exploitation of sex symbol filmstars – or what-have-you – is a view too restrictive to be acceptable to the writer for whom nothing human can be really foreign.

But my inability to accept all of Mr Herdman's opinions on 'the relationship which a national revival bears to the emergence of a national literature' doesn't prevent me from finding his work both provocative and (sometimes) profound.

Equally interesting is John Broom, on 'Some Neglected Scottish Novelists', an article which tells yet again the melancholy story of how quickly talented Scottish writers fall into oblivion.

That there is a direct relationship between this destructive process and the fact that in our schools and universities the study of literature is almost entirely the study of English literature scarcely needs stressing.

Among the more industrious labourers in the neglected vineyard of Scottish literary criticism is Tom Scott, who contributes to *Catalyst* a review of Sydney Goodsir Smith's recent collection, *Fifteen Poems and a Play*, where he finds 'the new note, the sombre deeper note, of the man who has suffered much and seen much he believed in, or tried to, shaken and battered'.

The poem which Dr Scott quotes as illustration for that remark is 'Said Heraclitus', of which he adds, 'In this poem ... I seem to sense a new and more serious Smith about to be born'.

Quite inadvertently, Dr Scott is describing what must be the longest literary pregnancy on record, for 'Said Heraclitus' appeared as long ago as 1951, in Mr Smith's privately printed pamphlet *The Aipple and the Hazel*. 'More serious' than some of Mr Smith's other work 'Said Heraclitus' may be, but to call it 'new' is entirely misleading.

To turn from Dr Scott's criticism to his creative work, he also contributes to *Catalyst* another poem in his fascinating series called 'Auld Sanct-Aundrians'.

This one, 'Broun the Butcher', has an essential 'coorseness' which may repel more delicately minded readers but can hardly fail to appeal to those with a liking for strong meat.

John Herdman (1941–). Novelist and prose writer.

Editor, *Catalyst*, 1970

A Truth Lover (Akros Publications 1973)

Memoirs of My Aunt Minnie and Clapperton (Rainbow Books 1974)

Pagan's Pilgrimage (Akros Publications 1978)

Imelda and Other Stories (Polygon 1993)

The Aipple and the Hazel Sydney Goodsir Smith (Caledonian Press 1951)

Fifteen Poems and a Play Sydney Goodsir Smith (Southside 1969)

Brand the Builder Tom Scott (The Ember Press 1975). This volume developed from the '*Auld Sanct-Aundrians*' sequence

18 October 1969

An alphabetic order of authors' names has resulted in George Mackay Brown heading the latest Scottish Arts Council list of publication awards, where he has received £300 for his most recent volume, *An Orkney Tapestry*.

But the book is of such exceptional quality that it probably deserves to feature first in the list for that much better reason too, since whatever the merits of the six other successful authors may be – and in some cases they are considerable – Mr Mackay Brown's writing is quite outstanding in its insight and sympathetic imagination.

His *Tapestry* has been woven out of his conviction that 'contemporary Orkney, cut off from the story of its past, is meaningless', and that modern Orcadians gain greater significance from an understanding of 'the terrible and fruitful things that actually happened to our ancestors'.

From these illuminating comprehensions has come what he modestly calls his 'attempt to get back to the roots and sources of the community, from which it draws its continuing life'.

Generous in acknowledgement of his sources, he states that he has had 'the help of the old stories, the old scrolls, the gathered legends, and the individual earth-rooted imagination', but no one can read the book without realising that the power of the author's own 'individual earth-rooted imagination' is the most energising force behind its weaving.

His aim has been 'to recount some of the events and imaginings that have made Orkney people what they are, in a sequence of vivid patterns', and his success is the result of his singular vividness of vision.

Beginning with a series of bird's-eye glimpses of landscape and folk, he then concentrates on how the communal life of shared centuries has shaped place and people in one particular valley, Rackwick, of which he writes a history that has all the qualities of legend.

The intertwining of prose and poetry in this chapter makes it an enchantment to read, even although the action is often tragic – 'evil is universal, and the simpler the society the starker it appears' – and the end is emptiness, with only one farm left operating in the whole valley.

For the dark irony involved in the kind of 'progress' which has resulted in the depopulation of those far islands, whose people were tempted 'to be nearer the source of all this affluence,' Mr Mackay Brown finds the desolate image of the deserted hearth.

> At Burnmouth the door hangs from a broken hinge
> And the fire is out.
>
> The windows of Shore empty sockets
> And the hearth coldness.
>
> The poor and the good fires are all quenched.

Even the little hope which the author can create with regard to the chance of families returning to Rackwick is scarcely less terrible than despair – 'It could happen that the atom-and-planet horror at the heart of our civilisation will scatter people again to the quiet beautiful fertile places of the world'.

But our civilisation has always had some horror at its heart, as Mr Mackay Brown's chapter on the Orkney Vikings, 'The Transfixed Dragon', shows him to be penetratingly aware in his poignant account of their plunderings and slaughters.

Against all expectation, however, that horror gave birth to holiness when the political murder of Earl Magnus was recognised as a martyrdom, and the new saint became the inspiration behind the building of Kirkwall Cathedral.

Mr Mackay Brown relates this marvellous story partly in narrative and partly in dramatic form, making it at once historical and contemporary with ourselves.

The traditional Orkney ballad, 'The Lady Odivere', is the occasion of a short story, 'The Ballad Singer', which is as illuminating as any Mr Mackay Brown has created; and his appreciation of the personality and the poetry of a remarkable Orcadian worthy of recent times, Robert Rendall, is written with unerring tact and generosity.

A miracle play, 'The Watcher', which concludes the volume, leaves one hoping that one day Mr Mackay Brown will attempt that drama about St Magnus which at present he feels he has 'not the ability' to write.

Your columnist, on the contrary, feels that Mr Mackay Brown has the ability to write magnificent prose and poetry about any and every aspect of Orkney life that seizes upon his imagination, and the grip which the St Magnus story exercises upon him is made evocatively evident in *An Orkney Tapestry.*

This is a splendid book, impossible to praise too highly or to read too often.

George Mackay Brown (1921–1996). Poet, novelist, short story writer and playwright.
An Orkney Tapestry (Victor Gollancz 1969)
Magnus (The Hogarth Press 1973)
Poems New and Selected (The Hogarth Press 1976)
Selected Poems 1954–1983 (John Murray 1991)
Robert Rendall (1898–1967). Poet and natural historian.
Country Sonnets (Kirkwall Press 1946)
An Island Shore – The Life and Work of Robert Rendall, Orkney poet and writer, edited by Neil Dickson, with a foreword by George Mackay Brown (The Orkney Press 1990)

25 October 1969

Kenneth Ireland, Director of Pitlochry Festival Theatre, has just asked me – along with everybody else, I expect, on the theatre's mailing list – to contribute towards the £50,000 which Pitlochry needs to raise before it can make preparations for next summer's season.

Mr Ireland ought to have remembered to remove my name from his mailing list at the same time as he wrote to George Bruce the producer of the BBC's *Arts Review* programme on Radio 4, informing him that I was no longer welcome in the Pitlochry Theatre.

If Mr Ireland seriously imagines that any theatre-goer, however enthusiastic, is likely to contribute cash to a dramatic enterprise from whose performances he has been banned, he must be the greatest innocent in show business.

But this particular ban came about not so much because I am an enthusiastic theatre-goer, but more because I am also a professional critic, paid to express my views on Pitlochry's productions (among other matters).

As such, it was my fate to be employed by the BBC to broadcast in the *Arts Review* programme for April on the subject of the opening play of the 1969 Pitlochry season, *The Queen's Highland Servant,* by William Douglas-Home, a piece of voguish Victoriana which – in my opinion – demonstrated abysmal ignorance of the Highland character.

In the course of my review of this work, I referred to Mr Home as 'a member of that Border family which is remarkable for its inability to spell its own surname' – a jest which derives from one of the best known stories in Scottish dramatic history.

This is the anecdote about how David Hume, the famous eighteenth century Edinburgh philosopher, in his last will and testament, left several bottles of wine to his friend, John Home, the then equally famous Edinburgh dramatist, on condition that Home would sign for them as 'Hume.'

By doing so, added the philosopher, the dramatist would remove the only point of difference which had ever divided them in the course of their acquaintance.

But this tale, familiar as it is to everybody who knows anything about 'Enlightenment' philosophy and drama, appears to be completely unknown to the Director of the Pitlochry Theatre, who seems to have regarded my reference to it as being personal attack on Mr William Douglas-Home in particular and his well-known relatives in general.

Under this uninformed misapprehension, Mr Ireland wrote to the producer of *Arts Review* banning me from his theatre, and since that time the BBC teams which have visited Pitlochry have been spared the embarrassment of my presence.

In those circumstances, Mr Ireland may rest assured that I shall spare him the further embarrassment of a contribution to Pitlochry's embarrassed finances, which are the result of a miscalculation of the income that the current season might bring in.

Artistically, that season has been one of the most praiseworthy in Pitlochry's frequently favourable record, with a wide-ranging variety of plays for which this column gave Mr Ireland every credit when theatre opened in the spring.

But this year, after several seasons when audiences kept on getting bigger and bigger, Pitlochry has been hit by what Mr Ireland calls 'rising costs and diminishing expenditure on entertainment generally', and even the expedient of higher seat prices has failed to bridge the gap between receipt and expenditure.

Even a critic banned from the Pitlochry Theatre must agree that 'it would be a disaster if it was forced to close down even for one season', and must do what he can to encourage theatre-goers who have not suffered the penalty of banning to express their appreciation of Pitlochry's past efforts by offering financial aid.

Drama enthusiasts will find a copy of Mr Ireland's appeal enclosed in the October issue of *Scottish Theatre*, a magazine which is itself appealing in quite a different sense.

Two articles in the current number are particularly thought-provoking – 'The Power Behind the Scenes', an analysis of the different sets of directors who control the destinies of Edinburgh's two 'sponsored' theatres, the Traverse and the Lyceum, and an interview with Bill Brown, the managing director of the STV on 'Television and the Theatre'.

While the Traverse directors (average age 35) are all amateur enthusiasts for the theatre, the Lyceum is dominated by town councillors (average age 55), even two of the four independent members being former members of Edinburgh Town Council – situations which go at least some distance towards explaining both the Traverse's occasional follies and the Lyceum's tendency to play safe.

The interview with Mr Brown shows that Scottish dramatists have little or nothing to hope for from STV except the chance to contribute scripts to *High Living*, which must surely be the lowest form of dramatic life outside Coronation Street.

Kenneth Ireland (1920–). Festival Director and Secretary, Pitlochry Festival Theatre 1957–1983.

William Douglas-Home (1912–1992). Author and playwright. Brother of Sir Alec Douglas-Home, Prime Minister 1963–1964. Plays include *The Secretary Bird* and *The Chiltern Hundreds*.

29 November 1969

If the name Alasdair Maclean is new to you, make a note of it, for it's bound to loom large across the landscape of contemporary Scottish letters.

Earlier this year Mr Maclean who is a 'mature student' at Edinburgh University, won first prize in the undergraduate poetry competition organised by the BBC's *University Notebook* programme.

Now the editor of *Lines Review*, Robin Fulton, presents no less than 21 of Mr Maclean's poems in the current issue, *Lines 30*, where he appears in the distinguished company of George Bruce and Stewart Conn (among others).

Rumour has it that Mr Maclean, who is now 43, began writing poetry only four years ago, and if rumour is not the usual lying jade this makes him a phenomenon.

Starting from scratch at an age when all too many poets lose their first fine careless rapture and lapse into silence, he has mastered his art in a brief period of time which most beginners would have found much too short for learning command.

In those four years Mr Maclean has found his own individual voice, a tone of quiet desperation which testifies to personal solitariness in a largely inimical world with an unstressed intensity far more moving than any 'song and dance.'

As in 'On Holiday in Ardnamurchan' –

No change. I find this land as hostile as my forebears did before the navvies drove their option through the hills.
My simple morning walks resented here.
Wind and tide reach for my throat; silence clings to me like brambles;
seaweed crosses rocks to trip me up and judging by the way it hesitates
the path knows what's in store for us.

There's no appeasing such implacability.

Combining a spare directness of style with the ability to make metaphors which are at once strikingly unusual and illuminatingly appropriate, Mr Maclean expresses human agony in poem after poem which blow down all the wind-breaks that we build between ourselves and the chilling gales of circumstance.

Three further poems by Mr Maclean appear in the current issue of *New Edinburgh Review*, a magazine of the arts and the sciences published six times a year by the Edinburgh University Student Publications Board.

Despite the title of the publishers, however, this is very far from being the usual student magazine, for the list of contributors is headed by the best known of science-publicists, Lord Ritchie Calder, and includes many members of the university staff.

Among these is Robin Fulton, recently appointed Writing Fellow at Edinburgh in succession to Norman MacCaig – a well-deserved award to a writer who has not only made his own valuable individual contribution to modern Scottish poetry but has helped many others to appear in print, first as editor of *Lines* and now as poetry editor of this new university publication.

Perhaps even more remarkable than Mr Fulton's talent is his modesty, for although he has been editor of *Lines* for more than two years only one of his own poems has appeared in some half-dozen numbers of the magazine, and his own verse is again conspicuous by its absence from *New Edinburgh Review*.

Instead, he gives us an article on three other writers, George Mackay Brown, Iain Crichton Smith and Gordon Williams, who were short-listed for the Scottish Arts Council's £1,000 fiction prize.

In the event, the prize was given to Mr Mackay Brown, and Mr

Fulton – writing before the award was announced – makes that result appear inevitable, such is the subtlety and sympathetic skill of his analysis of the Orcadian author's short story collection, *A Time to Keep*.

Yet Mr Fulton does justice to the virtues of Mr Crichton Smith's 'historical' novelette, *Consider the Lilies*, and Mr Williams's 'autobiographical' novel, *From Scenes Like These*, with a generous acumen which counterpoints his severity on what he considers to be their faults.

This is literary criticism of a high order, unclouded by the coteries coat trailing which raises so much dust to befog contemporary reviewing, and it is good to see that Mr Fulton's article is to be followed by others under the same general title of 'Argus'.

At only two shillings a copy, *New Edinburgh Review* is the biggest magazine bargain now in print. It can be ordered from 1 Buccleuch Place, Edinburgh.

Lines Review – now published from Edgefield Road, Loanhead, Midlothian – has a subscription of 16s, for four issues, which once again represents remarkable economy.

Both are essential for anyone desirous of keeping abreast of literary developments in Scotland.

Alasdair Maclean (1926–1994). Poet.
From the Wilderness (Victor Gollancz 1973)
Waking the Dead (Victor Gollancz 1976)

Iain Crichton Smith (*Iain Mac A'Ghobhainn*) (1928–). Poet, novelist, short-story writer and playwright in Gaelic and English.
Consider the Lilies (Victor Gollancz 1968)
Selected Poems, 1955–1980 edited by Robin Fulton (Macdonald 1981)
Selected Poems (Carcanet 1985)
Collected Poems (Carcanet 1992)

Gordon Williams (1934–). Novelist and journalist.
From Scenes Like These (Secker and Warburg 1968) was shortlisted for the Booker Prize and made into a film under the title *Straw Dogs, the Siege of Trencher's Farm* in 1969.

New Edinburgh Review. Established 1969. Published by Edinburgh University Student Publications Board; various editors; later renamed *Edinburgh Review*, a bi-annual journal under the Edinburgh University Press imprint, 22 George Square, Edinburgh at an annual subscription of £15.

Lines Review is still published quarterly from the same address, for a current annual subscription of £10.

20 December 1969

Twenty-eight years after the death of the author of *Hamewith*, Charles Murray, the publication of his *Last Poems* by Aberdeen University Press serves as a reminder that this Strathdon scriever was at one and the same time the most popular Scottish poet of his period with the public in general, and the least regarded versifier of his age among those of his younger contemporaries, who either wrote verse or wrote about it in the critical reviews.

In Hugh MacDiarmid's anthology, *The Golden Treasury of Scottish Poetry* (1940), Murray is represented only by his early poem on an Aberdeenshire childhood, 'The Whistle', and Maurice Lindsay's selection, *Modern Scottish Poetry* (1946), omits him.

Yet Murray is not only a notable poet in himself, he is also a highly significant figure in the history of Scots poetry, for in the work which he produced between 1893 and 1920 the reader can see the poetry emerging from the nineteenth century rural parish and its parochial concerns and attempting – with more success than Murray has ever been given credit for – to grapple with the wider and wilder themes of the twentieth century world.

In his early *Hamewith* poems it is a source of strength, as well as one of the reasons for his limited range, that the work is rooted in the everyday realities of a regional community.

While his exploration of character may not go deep – he never penetrates the secret places of the heart or the subtler reaches of the intellect – his observation of external behaviour is both exact and pointed, whether he shows his country folk at work or at play, the Packman rising by hard graft and sharp practice to become Agent of the bank, the miller roaring home fou from the fair.

The pointedness of those poems is due to Murray sharing the humour of the characters he presented, the sly, sardonic, 'afftakkin' wit, the joke with a sting in its tail.

His more personal early poems, expressing his own nostalgia for the Scottish scene which he had left behind in order to seek his fortune in foreign parts, are less successful, for Murray is the kind of writer who needs a persona, a mask, another man's mouth to speak through, before he himself can speak without self-consciousness or strain.

When he writes in the first person about the Scotland of long ago and far away, he becomes so embarrassed at giving away his feelings – and here, of course, as everywhere else, he is the Aberdonian *par excellence* – that he starts striking awkward attitudes which are more embarrassing still and produces blush-making blurb about 'the auld dear kirk, the dear auld hame'.

More than one modern critic has found much of Murray's work to be pedestrian, or prosaic, a view which takes insufficient heed of TS Eliot's remark, 'To have the virtues of good prose is the first and minimum requirement of good poetry'.

With Murray's impeccable ear for the rhythm and cadence and idiom of Aberdeenshire speech, his verse almost always possesses this 'minimum requirement', although it seldom possesses any more than this, and hardly ever takes 'the mad leap into the symbol' to create that simultaneous flash when energy of rhythm, vividness of image, and sheer stab of feeling combine to flood the eyes with tears or bristle the hair on the nape of the neck – the inexplicable experience which is poetry at its most potent and most pure.

The first of Murray's war poems are tub-thumping patriotism of the most blatant vulgarity – like most non-combatants at the beginning, he was misled by popular jingoism – but 'Dockens Afore his Peers', which belongs to 1916, is the best of all his dramatic monologues, an ironically acute study of provincial chicanery and self-interest triumphing over national necessity, a poem so topical that it must have come red-hot off the press.

The same is true of the finest of his Scots versions of Horace, *Parcus deorem*, published in 1920, where the original Latin verses are transformed into brilliantly savage satire on the War and its aftermath, the flu epidemic, the food queues, the abdication of the Kaiser and the Russian Revolution – and where the concluding image is as topical as a bombing raid.

> An' Fortune like an aeroplane comes loopin' doon the blue,
> An' kills a Czar to place in pooer some raggit Russian Jew.

If Murray's war-time poems are still more sardonic than those that made his early reputation, they are stronger too, even more tightly-knit, succinct, concentrated, economical.

Charles Murray (1864–1941). Poet and civil engineer.
> *The Last Poems* Preface and notes by Alexander Keith. Appreciation by Nan Shepherd (Aberdeen University Press for the Charles Murray Memorial Trust 1969)
> *Hamewith – The Complete Poems of Charles Murray* edited by Nan Shepherd. (Aberdeen University Press for the Charles Murray Memorial Trust 1979)

27 December 1969

Duncan Glen, the editor of *Akros*, has bid fair to out-internationalise *Scottish International* in his current number.

An article on the Anglo–Welsh verse renaissance, two articles on the contemporary poetry scene in England, eight poems from Wales and twelve from English writers – all of these, alongside four articles on Scottish themes and fifteen poems from Scotland, demonstrate that Mr Glen's range of interest is as wide as that of any editor in the country.

The healthy concern with artistic activities in societies other than our own which the Scottish arts magazines have expressed in recent issues is a sign of strength, if – as in Mr Glen's case – it springs from sufficient confidence in our own identity to wish to see that in a wider context.

Such is the standard of the Scottish poems in *Akros 12*, both in Scots and in English, that we need fear comparison with no one.

By publishing no less than eight Scots poems by Alastair Mackie, Mr Glen has given him the opportunity to show the scintillating scope of his talent, from the acrid wit of 'In Absentia' ('We've no heard frae God this while') to the shuddering desolation of 'Pietà'; from the dazzling images of 'New Moon' to the colloquial directness of 'Drappit'. A Scots poet whose name is new to me, Donald Campbell, uses a similar colloquial style in 'Man o the Warld', as does Mr Glen himself in 'Innocence', while TS Law in 'The Wurld We Tyne' reaches beyond it in a moving attempt to explore the complexities of the relationships between self and scene.

In English, Edwin Morgan's 'Afterwards' weaves a pattern of unusual, individual and highly sensuous images into an indictment of war all the more effective for the indirectness of his approach. Maurice Lindsay's 'The Vacant Chair' bridges the generation gap in a way which is at once witty and unexpected, and Rory Watson's 'Stones' is as striking in the novelty of its technique as in the force of its impact.

Compared with the poems, the articles from Scotland are disappointing, apart from the editor's own essay on Hugh MacDiarmid's 'divine wisdom' poems, 'The Word which Silence Speaks', a gallant effort to express the inexpressible.

But the pieces on Robert Garioch and Kenneth White are uncritical puffs, Donald Campbell on 'Why Scots?' is too slight to be of much general interest, and Tom Scott's view of the Scottish tradition as 'continuous because it belongs not to time but eternity' is transcendental tarradiddle, the kind of chauvinistic shamanism which brings concern with Scottish letters into disrepute.

For Mr Glen's own concern with Scottish letters, however, there can only be gratitude and praise and the hope that *Akros* will long continue its present policy of offering space to writers of every school and all kinds of attitudes.

With a subscription of 15s. for 4 copies, *Akros* is published 3 times a year, in January, April and August, from 14 Parklands Avenue, Penwortham, Preston, Lancashire – for Mr Glen (to our shame be it said) is yet another Scot who has had to exile himself in order to earn a living.

As well as acting as editor, Mr Glen is also the poet who writes under the pseudonym of 'Ronald Eadie Munro' and presents a selection of his recent work in the latest volume of the Modern Scottish Poets series published by Caithness Books, *Kythings*.

Usually I'm more irritated than impressed by the number of *noms-de-plume* on the Scottish literary scene, but in Duncan Ronald Eadie Glen Munro's case the use of a pen-name can be justified, or at least excused, on the argument that two poets are represented in *Kythings* rather than simply one.

First there is Duncan Glen, who writes autobiographical poems about the actualities of his own experience, as in 'My Faither', an elegy of such profound simplicity that it is almost an impertinence to comment on its skill, or in 'Ceremonial', where the sight of a dead mouse leads to an appreciation of the intermingledom of 'the bricht colours o life and daith' expressed with a delicate restraint which still contains both pity and affirmation.

Then there is Munro – a name chosen for its association with Scottish summits? – who writes visionary poems on his relationship with the Muse, where sky imagery combines and contrasts with images of 'glaur' and brute vitality in his striving to express the paradoxical association of idealism with the foulest fact.

None of these latter poems seems to me entirely successful, for their sense is sometimes as clouded as the skies that arch over their maker, but they bear witness to an endeavour to interweave the actual with the imaginative which is all the more admirable for the infrequency with which post-renaissance poetry in Scots has made the attempt.

Mr Glen's Scots medium reads like a living language, not a literary lingo, and he handles it with an apparently easy command which augurs well for his future.

Donald Campbell (1940–). Poet, playwright, and theatre historian.
Rhymes 'N Reasons, with an Introduction by Hugh MacDiarmid (Reprographia 1972)
Selected Poems 1970–1990 (Galliard 1990)

His best known plays include *The Jesuit* (1976), *The Widows of Clyth* (1978), *The Fisher Boy And The Honest Lass* (1990) and *The Ould Fella* (1993).

Duncan Glen (1933–). Poet, editor and publisher.

Kythings (under pseudonym Ronald Eadie Munro) (Caithness Books 1969)
In Appearances (Akros Publications 1971)
Realities - Poems (Akros Publications 1980)
Selected Poems 1965-1990 (Akros Publications 1991)
Editor *Akros* magazine 1965-1983, when it ceased publication.
Sole proprietor of Akros Publications which since 1965 has produced just under 200 titles in pamphlet, paperback and hardback format that reads like an extensive bibliography of contemporary Scottish poetry. He now operates from 33 Lady Nairn Avenue, Kirkcaldy.

28 February 1970

If this column were asked to suggest a candidate for an award for personal initiative in the arts, one of the first names to come to mind would be that of Kenneth Roy, editor of the monthly magazine *Scottish Theatre*.

To found a Scottish magazine with no finance behind it except one's own resources, and to keep it alive for a twelvemonth, is a task beside which the labours of Hercules appear puny.

Our recent literary past is littered with the corpses of periodicals which, leaping into life in a fine flush of youth, have rapidly sickened as a result of the financial famine caused by public disinterest, and collapsed and died so prematurely as to leave scarcely a memory behind.

At a time when Scottish theatre is in the slough of despond, only someone whose courage brimmed over into foolhardiness could have seen a way to ensure success for a monthly devoted to the drama in Scotland, and only someone whose competence was as notable as his determination could have transformed his vision into an enduring reality.

That Kenneth Roy is such a man is proved beyond any dispute by the fact that the present issue of *Scottish Theatre* is the twelfth monthly number, with a wide range of contributions from such variously distinguished theatrical personalities as Lindsay Anderson, Ivor Brown, JC Trewin and – coming nearer home – George Bruce, Christopher Small, Robert Trotter and Allen Wright.

Unlike a number of Scottish publications which appear less and less frequently, *Scottish Theatre* contrives to sell at the astonishingly reasonable price of half-a-crown, and yet receives no subsidy whatever from the Scottish Arts Council.

Considering that *Scottish Theatre* has been consistently readable, whereas the magazine which receives the Council's biggest financial backing, *Scottish International,* has too often swung dizzily to and fro between the unattractive extremes of the dull and daft, there appears to be more rhyme than reason in the situation.

As if to put the Arts Council to shame for its dilatoriness in recognising worth-while endeavour, *Scottish Theatre*'s editor has now set another arrow to his bow and announced the quarterly publication of 'a series of plays, new or hitherto unpublished, by Scottish dramatists or dramatists living in Scotland.'

The first of these, to be issued in paperback on 15 March , will be *Seven Characters Out of the Dream,* 'a comedy for seven costumes left over from a Shakespearean production,' by the Glasgow dramatist, Joan Ure.

That there is such widespread ignorance of the work of our native dramatists here is largely – perhaps chiefly – due to the fact that plays designed in the first place for Scottish audiences have had slight financial attraction for London publishers, with the regrettable result that only the most minuscule of minorities have ever appeared in print.

Probably the most notable of our unpublished dramatic *chefs d'oeuvres* is Robert McLellan's masterpiece, *Jamie the Saxt,* which had to wait for more than 30 years to be transferred from stage to page.

At long last, however, this too will achieve publication in 1970, as one of the first three volumes in the Scottish Library series published by Messrs Calder and Boyars.

The initiative behind this particular enterprise has been not so much personal as in Kenneth Roy's case – as co-operative on the part of the scholars who have banded together as the Universities' Committee in Scottish Literature and made a start (with Arts Council help) at the gigantic task of filling the huge gaps in the publication of worthwhile Scottish prose, poetry and drama.

As secretary of this organisation, it has been my pleasantly surprising experience to discover that the old adage about committees never getting anything done can be given the lie by the other popular proverb about a will and a way.

That a single determined will can make a way for a whole movement has been demonstrated indisputably by Hugh MacDiarmid, the genius who found Scottish poetry in the doldrums and has lifted it to the heights.

At the head of the Scottish Arts Council's recent list of grants to writers resident in Scotland was a 'Special Award' of £1,000 to Hugh

MacDiarmid.

While his services to Scottish poetry have been quite priceless, it is heart-warming to find that on this occasion, at least, the prophet has not been without honour in his own country.

The award does honour to the Scottish Arts Council, too.

Kenneth Roy (1945–). Author, publisher, journalist and broadcaster. Editor, *Scottish Theatre* magazine 1969–1972. Presenter/Interviewer BBC Reporting Scotland 1972–1980. Managing Director, West Sound Radio 1980-1982.

Travels in a Small Country (Carrick Media 1989)

The Closing Head Lines – Inside Scottish Broadcasting (Carrick Media 1993)

Robert McLellan (1907–1985). Playwright and poet.

The best known of his plays are *Jamie the Saxt* (1938), *Torwatletie* (1946), and *The Flouers o Edinburgh* (1948).

Joan Ure, pseudonym of Elizabeth Clark (1919-1978). Playwright.

Five Short Plays (Scottish Society of Playwrights 1979)